MAKING
MEAD
(HONEY WINE)

D1528343

MAKING MEAD
(HONEY WINE)

History, Recipes, Methods and Equipment

ROGER A. MORSE

Professor of Apiculture ◍ Cornell University ◍ Ithaca, N.Y.

WICWAS PRESS

Published by Wicwas Press

Designed by Mary A. Scott

Library of Congress Catalog Card Number: 80-53765
ISBN: 1-878075-04-7
ISBN: 978-1-878075-04-8

Contents

Preface 9
I. Mead — What Is It? 11
   Alcohol is a natural product 13
   Government classification of alcoholic beverages 15
   The history of mead 16
   Good references on ancient mead making 17
   Names for mead 22
   The current status of honey drinks 23
II. Honey 25
   Nectar 26
   Making nectar into honey 27
   Crystallized honey 28
   Growth factors in honey............................ 30
   Pollen in honey 30
   The effect of filtration on honey 31
   Comb and brood in mead making 31
   Cappings honey 32
   The effect of diluting honey 33
   The special keeping quality of honey 33
III. Equipment for Mead Making 34
   Sanitation 35
   Barrels, carboys and jugs 37
   Fermentation valves................................ 40

6 CONTENTS

Temperature control 42
IV. Yeasts and the Fermentation 44
The best yeast for mead 45
Yeast cells 46
The ecology of yeast cell growth 47
Yeast starters and their propagation 48
Dried yeast cultures 50
The osmophilic yeasts............................. 51
Sulfur and sulfiting wines 53
Antifoams 54
V. Recipes and Formulas............................ 57
Mead 58
Metheglin.. 62
Fruit meads 64
Hops in mead making 65
Boiling the honey-water mixture 66
VI. Fermenting, Racking and Aging.................. 68
The primary fermentation 69
The first racking 71
The second and subsequent rackings................ 73
Stuck meads...................................... 74
Aging 75
Meads that will not clear 77
VII. Bottling and Closures 80
Bottles.. 80
Headspace 82
Screw caps 83
Crown caps 83
Corks and corking 85
Capsules and foils 92
Labels 92
VIII. Sparkling Mead 94
History 95
The base for a sparkling mead 97
How to make sparkling mead...................... 97

Disgorging and sweetening 101
Drinking sparkling meads 105
IX. Diseases and Disorders 107
Vinegar bacteria 108
Ropiness in mead................................. 109
Metallic cloudiness and sediments 110
Protein precipitate 110
X. Home Analysis and Judging 112
Residual sugar 113
Hydrometers 115
Alcohol... 115
Total solids in a must............................ 118
Measuring pH................................... 118
Total and volatile acidity 119
Judging mead 123
Index... 126

Preface

Keeping bees may lead one to the pursuit of many avocations, from making candles to producing mead. I became interested in mead production in 1950. At that time, honey prices were depressed. Beekeepers had expanded their operations during the Second World War, when sugar was scarce; when sugar again became plentiful, the price of honey fell. We investigated mead making, thinking it might be a way to use the surplus honey in the country.

Professor Otto Rohn was the first to give me some practical suggestions and to assist me in finding references on the subject. He selected several yeasts from his famous collection for me to test. One of these has been reserved by Professor Steinkraus and myself to be used with the patent we hold on making mead.

This book is designed to assist those who wish to make mead at home. Readers will find I've injected some prejudice into the manuscript. I prefer well-aged meads. I like corked bottles better than those stopped with a plastic or crown cap. I even suggest that those who wish to present a superior product for their own and their friends' consumption should design a good label for the bottle.

Many people have assisted me in the preparation of this manuscript, and I thank them for their interest and assistance. My father, Dr. Grant D. Morse, who gave me my first hive of bees when I was ten years old, read the manuscript and made suggestions. Professor Emeritus E. S. Phillips, former Editor of the American Wine Society Journal and himself a well-known author, also made suggestions on the manuscript and was kind enough to give some of the illustrations. Professor K. H. Steinkraus, with whom I have written several papers on mead and honey, likewise reviewed my pages and made suggestions. Beth French typed the manuscript, shortened sentences, and clarified some phrases that make the whole thing more readable. I also thank my secretary, Lois Bower, who has assisted in the preparation of many drafts and herself offered suggestions that have aided in the preparation of this book.

I.
Mead—
What Is It?

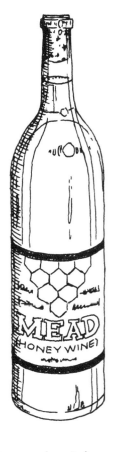

Mead is honey wine. It is made when honey is diluted and allowed to ferment. Mead is thought by many to have been the first alcoholic beverage made by man; there are many reasons why this might be true. Ancient men in Europe and Africa had no sugar[1] and relatively few fruits. In fact, the diets of people of the Egyptian, Greek, and Roman Empires, even at their peaks, were poor by our standards. Honey was not only of prime importance as a sweet, but it was one of the few things from which an alcoholic beverage could be made.

In reviewing the older literature on honey wine, two facts are apparent: (1) many of the meads were sweet, and (2) many were strongly spiced. I detect a positive trend away from sweet and spiced meads and wines today. I have a strong suspicion, too, that extra honey and spices were often used to cover up faulty fermentations; this is not an unreasonable hypothesis, since it was only a little over 100 years ago that the French scientist Pasteur investigated wine making and discovered the yeast cell. Before Pasteur's work,[2] wine and mead makers had no notion what caused a fermentation, and their methods were crude and often erroneous.

While sugar is the chief food for the yeast cell, yeasts need vitamins, minerals, and certain elements to grow, reproduce, and make alcohol. Honey contains only a limited amount of nutrients, and these are further reduced because the honey must be diluted to conduct a fermentation. The lack of nutrients

---

[1]The history of sugar is interesting to explore. Sugar cane comes to us from the South Pacific. The Chinese are credited with building the first sugar mill in about 200 B.C., but it was not until the Islamic invasion of the Mediterranean area in about 600 A.D. that sugar cane was introduced to the people living in that area. It took at least 800 years for men to carry sugar cane from China to Europe! This, too, explains why there are so many biblical references to honey it was the only common sweet available to people at the time the Bible was written.

At the time of the American Revolutionary War, there was still little sugar produced in America, and per capita consumption was about 12 pounds per year. In the mid 1800's it had risen to about 50 pounds per person per year, still far short of the nearly 140 pounds it is today. These data explain, too, why beekeeping was so important to the American colonists and others at that time. Presumably people then had as much of a sweet tooth as they have today; honey was a dear commodity.

[2]It is interesting that in the United States we associate Pasteur with the process of pasteurizing milk. In France and most of the rest of the world, he is honored for his research on wine.

slows the fermentation and increases the danger of wine disease. Honey has the right degree of acidity (pH) for a fermentation, but it is low in acid; dilution of the honey also dilutes the acid and thus the resulting wine may be bland. This may be why fruit juice, which is usually high in acid, was often combined with the honey by old time mead makers.

Recipes for making mead are discussed in detail later. Very fine meads with an excellent flavor can be made if simple rules are followed: It is important to add nutrients so that the fermentation can be conducted within a reasonable period of time; it is necessary to add acid to enhance the flavor and keeping qualities of the product; modern technology must be used to stop the growth of harmful organisms; the new mead must be aged; and, last, it must be properly bottled to retain its delicate flavor. How all this is done is the subject of this book.

Alcohol is a natural product

Ethyl alcohol (drinking alcohol) is a natural product. It is made when yeast cells ingest sugar, use about five per cent for their own metabolism and growth, and discard the remainder as carbon dioxide and alcohol. Carbon dioxide and alcohol are yeast cell waste products. Yeast cells do not set out by design to produce alcohol. They consume sugar (and nutrients) to live and survive. They are inefficient in their use of sugar, and this is to man's benefit.

From a practical point of view, two parts of sugar will result in production of one part of alcohol and one part of carbon dioxide. The conversion is not precisely two to one, and actually a 22 per cent sugar solution will produce about a 12 per cent solution of alcohol. The percentages are affected by temperature and other conditions under which the yeast cells are grown.

Yeast cells, like any living organism, need vitamins, minerals, and sundry nutrients. While sugar is their chief food, they cannot grow and produce carbon dioxide and alcohol without a balanced diet. The better the diet, the more rapidly the fermentation will proceed. In general, we encourage rapid fermentations because the alcohol content will protect the final product against other yeasts, bacteria, molds, and fungi that cause off-flavor or disease. In fact, the production of alcohol through fermentation is said to be a natural method of preserving a fruit juice.

When I first began to read about wine and mead making, I was impressed by the story about two wine connoisseurs, one of whom complained the wine they were tasting had a copper flavor while the second said it also tasted of shoe leather. Upon draining the flask, they found a cobbler's nail and this settled the question.

Such stories abound and are first-class humbug. Still, there are among us those who have more discriminating palates. In wine tasting sessions this becomes apparent, though occasionally an individual may change a group's minds, just as the occasional juror has been known to reverse the decision of the majority of his peers.

In tasting wine or mead it is most important to recognize obvious off-flavors, such as those produced by an acetic acid fermentation or by the presence of too much tannin, or the bland taste of an overaged product. Beyond that, one must be careful about treading upon the taste preferences of others. I remember distinctly the first time I ever tasted the Greek retsina. It is a wine to which pine resin is added after the fermentation, and it has a decided resinous taste. I was horrified. Several weeks later, I purchased a bottle because I was not certain whether my first impression was right or wrong. I was wrong, and have since decided that, as something different, one might enjoy a glass about once every two or three years. Retsina is best with heavier foods, especially those with a great deal of olive oil. However, one must not think of it as a wine; it is a different beverage.

Government classification of alcoholic beverages

Alcoholic beverages usually fall into five classes: beer, wine, fortified wines, cordials and liqueurs, and distilled spirits such as whiskey and gin. For tax purposes, the United States government makes further sub-divisions as follows (I think many people are not aware of the extent to which their government organizes, reorganizes, and takes their money!):

Beverage	Tax Basis	Current Tax Rate (dollars)
Still wines		
(not more than 14% alcohol)	Wine gal.	0.17
(more than 14% but not exceeding 21% alcohol)	Wine gal.	0.67
(more than 21% but not exceeding 24% alcohol)	Wine gal.	2.28
(more than 24% alcohol)	Same as distilled spirits	
Artificially carbonated wine	Gallon	2.40
Champagne	Gallon	3.40
Wine cordials and liqueurs[3]	Gallon	1.92
Distilled spirits (whiskeys and gins)	Gallon	10.50
Beer	Barrel	9.00

---

[3]Distilled spirits used to fortify wines, liqueurs, and cordials are taxed an additional 30¢ per proof gallon. Proof is defined as "the ethyl alcohol content of a liquid at 60°F. stated as twice the per cent of ethyl alcohol by volume" (our government's words); an 80 proof beverage contains 40 per cent alcohol.

The history of mead

Writing about history is a difficult task. Early in my investigations into mead making, at a time when there was a surplus of honey[4] and we were seeking ways to dispose of it, I looked into mead's history, thinking that the use of mead by a historical character might be used in commercial promotion. Since mead was presumably popular in Robin Hood's time, I thought he might be a logical character to study. I started by checking my childrens' books, only to find that we owned two books entitled *Robin Hood,* by two different authors. I searched further and found that many people had written the story of Robin Hood; though written by different authors, all the books contained the same stories and characters. Looking still further, I found Professor F. J. Child's *English and Scottish Ballads;* volume 6, 1859, is devoted to Robin Hood. Professor Child, in his introduction, makes it clear that while Robin Hood is a well-known hero, he probably never lived. King Richard did exist, and he was an unpopular king; he went on crusades to the Holy Land because they were the only wars his people would support. His high taxes made many people into outlaws, hunted by Prince John, who collected the money to support his brother's shenanigans. The tales of Robin Hood were first set on paper about 1362, some 160 to 180 years after Robin Hood was presumed to have lived. Professor Child suggests that, given time and the passing of lyrics from one ballad singer to another, "Robin Hood" became the popular name assigned to all outlaws who took from the rich and gave to the poor during those hard times. I mention all this only to show that many things in history that

---

[4]During the Second World War the number of honey bee colonies and honey production were increased. When sugar became plentiful and cheap after the war, the price of honey fell. At one time the Fingerlakes Honey Producers Cooperative in New York State held over two million pounds of buckwheat honey for more than two years because they could not dispose of it at any price.

we think are true are not; we can only guess at how honey wine was made before the 1600's.

I read the old Robin Hood ballads, as recorded by Child, and came to the conclusion that those who set them down were as graceful with the English language as our writers are today. I am especially fond of the following lines on the meeting of Robin Hood and Little John and their fight on the "long, narrow bridge":

> O then into fury the stranger he grew,
> And gave him a damnable look.
> And with it a blow that laid him full low,
> And tumbled him into the brook.

But was honey wine among the items Robin Hood stole from Prince John, the sheriff, and other notables? The ballads do not prove this one way or the other. At one point I read in Child's work that Robin Hood took "met and met"; I am willing to settle for those old English words meaning "meat and mead" and to state unequivocally, and with as much authority as many historians, that Robin Hood did steal and drink mead, and that he would be an excellent character around whom to build a promotion program for honey wine.

Good references on ancient mead making

We know that two to five thousand years ago people in the Egyptian, Greek and Roman empires made honey wine. We also know that people in England made mead as early as the Roman invasion of their land. There are also many tales of Norsemen making wine from honey and some suggestion that perhaps they toasted one another with mead drunk from the skulls of their slain enemies. Between 1000 and 1400 A.D. mead became even more famous, and both the English and Poles made great quantities of it. We know little about their beekeeping techniques, except that they were crude, and even less about how they made their drink.[5]

The best reference I know on how mead was really made in olden times is: *The Closet of the Eminently Learned Sir Kenelme Digbie Kt. Opened: Whereby is Discovered Several Ways for Making of Metheglin, Sider, Cherry-Wine, &c together with Excellent Directions for Cookery: As also for Preserving, Conserving, Candying, &c.* This book was published in 1669 in English; Digbie lived between 1603 and 1665. While this is not an ancient reference, it is older and better documented than most. The book was reprinted in 1910 by Anne Macdonell, who wrote a romantic introduction concerning Digbie's travels, exploits, and importance.

Three recipes from Digbie's book are given below.

1. **"A Receipt to Make Metheglin as It is Made at Liege, Communicated by Mr. Masillon**

    Take one Measure of Honey, and three Measures of Water, and let it boil till one measure be boiled away, so that there be left three measures in all; as for Example, take to one Pot of Honey, three Pots of Water, and let it boil so long, till it come to three Pots. During which time you must Skim it very well as soon as any scum riseth; which you are to continue till there rise no scum more. You may, if you please, put to it some spice, to wit, Cloves and Ginger; the quantity of which is to be proportioned according as you will have your Meath, strong or weak. But this you do before it begin to boil. There are some that put either Yeast of Beer, or Leaven of bread into it, to make it work. But this is not necessary at all; and much less to set it into the Sun. Mr. Masillon doth neither the one nor the other. After-

---

[5]An annotated bibliography by the author on honey wine, including references to many of the ancient methods and books on the history of mead and mead making, is available by writing International Bee Research Association, Hill House, Gerrards Cross, Bucks, SL9 ONR, England.

wards for to Tun[6] it, you must let it grow Luke-warm, for to advance it. And if you do intend to keep your Meathe a long time, you may put into it some hopps of this fashion. Take to every Barrel of Meathe a Pound of Hops without leaves, that is, of Ordinary Hops used for Beer but well cleansed, taking only the Flowers, without the Green-leaves and stalks. Boil this pound of Hops in a Pot and half of fair water, till it come to one Pot, and this quantity is sufficient for a Barrel of Meathe. A Barrel at Liege holdeth ninety Pots, and a Pot is as much as a Wine quart in England. (I have since been informed from Liege, that a Pot of that Countrey holdeth 48 Ounces of Apothecary's measure; which I judge to be a Pottle according to London measure, or two Winequarts.) When you Tun your Meath, you must not fill your Barrel by half a foot, that so it may have room to work. Then let it stand six weeks slightly stopped; which being expired, if the Meath do not work, stop it up very close. Yet must you not fill up the Barrel to the very brim. After six Months you draw off the clear into another Barrel, or strong Bottles, leaving the dregs, and filling up your new Barrel, or Bottels, and stopping it or them very close.

The Meath that is made this way, (*Viz*. In the Spring, in the Month of April or May, which is the proper time for making of it,) will keep many a year."

2. **"Hydromel as I Made It Weak for The Queen Mother**
Take 18 quarts of spring-water, and one quart of honey; when the water is warm, put the honey into it. When it boileth up, skim it very well, and continue skimming it, as long as any scum will rise. Then put in one Race of Ginger (sliced in thin slices,) four Cloves, and a little sprig of green Rosemary. Let these boil in the Liquor so long, till in all it have boiled one hour. Then set it to cool, till it be blood-

---

[6]My 1859 Webster's says to tun is to put into casks; in Germany a Tun is a cask, usually a large one.

warm; and then put to it a spoonful of Ale-yest. When it is worked up, put it into a vessel of a fit size; and after two or three days, bottle it up. You may drink it after six weeks, or two moneths.

Thus was the Hydromel made that I gave the Queen, which was exceedingly liked by everybody."

3. "A Receipt for Meathe

To seven quarts of water, take two quarts of honey, and mix it well together; then set it on the fire to boil, and take three or four Parsley-roots, and as many Fennel-roots, and shave them clean, and slice them, and put them into the Liquor, and boil altogether, and skim it very well all the while it is a boyling; and when there will no more scum rise, then it is boiled enough; but be careful that none of the scum do boil into it. Then take it off, and let it cool till the next day. Then put it up in a close vessel, and put thereto half a pint of new good barm, and a very few Cloves pounded and put in a Linnen-cloth, and tie it in a vessel, and stop it up close; and within a fortnight, it will be ready to drink: but if it stay longer, it will be the better."

We learn much from these three recipes. Perhaps most important is that while yeast might be used, and space left at the top of the barrel for an active fermentation, the relationship among yeast, alcohol, and carbon dioxide was not clear. Sanitation was lacking and no doubt many of the fermentations were faculty.

It is obvious too that boiling the honey-water mixture was a common practice. We know today that the chief value of boiling is that is causes the proteins to precipitate; without boiling, the final product is not clear. However, since people then did not understand pasteurization any more than they did fermentation, this does not explain why the early recipes call for boiling.

We can also determine that scarcely a mead was made without adding spice. Our understanding today is that metheglin is spiced and mead is not; the situation 300 years ago is not so clear. Hops were added frequently; they aid in clarification, and are discussed more fully in chapter V.

Measures and measuring were obviously a problem 300 years ago, since there was little standardization. One must be careful not to assume that measures and methods suggested even 50 or 100 years ago are the same as they are today.

Edward Bevan,[7] an Englishman writing in 1827, indicated that in his day mead was seldom made, and held "a very humble rank" among our imperfect vinous productions. He felt that either the ancients had a very unpampered taste or they had not handed down their better methods of mead making. Probably his first thought is more correct, and it is probably that the earlier peoples, knowing nothing else, were more than satisfied with the drink that they then made from honey. However, as soon as European grape wine became common, and as the people in Southern Europe improved their methods of fermentation one hundred to three hundred years ago, these beverages moved into northern Europe and soon became very popular. There is no question that grape juice, with its almost perfect mix of sugar, acid, and nutrients, is an easy medium to use to make an alcoholic drink; making an equally good mead requires much care.

Those who wish to pursue the history of mead more fully will find G. R. Gayre's *Wassail! in Mazers of Mead* (Phillimore and Co. Ltd., London, 1948) an interesting and valuable reference. Gayre starts with a chapter on honey and mead in mythology. He then discusses mead's use among the ancient people with emphasis on northern Europe; this chapter is followed by one on mead in the Middle Ages up to the eighteenth century. The reasons the use of mead declined is next, followed by a

[7]Bevan, Edward, 1827. *The Honey-bee, its Natural History, Physiology and Management.* Baldwin, Cradock and Joy, London. 404 pages.

discussion of the names of honey drinks. His last chapters include thoughts on mead's qualities, and how it should be drunk. Gayre was head of a short-lived company that attempted, immediately after the Second World War, to revive the use of mead in England.

Names for mead

Most dictionaries I have checked say in very simple terms that mead is honey wine. Various spellings have been used, especially in England, including med, met, meath, meathe, and meda. One dictionary I have says mead is an alcoholic liquor made from honey and water; the same book says a liquor is usually a distilled beverage. I am inclined to agree that the term liquor does suggest distillation. I think they used the term alcoholic liquor because they were prompted by some wine purist. Many such people would like to use the term wine only for a beverage made from grapes.

There are a great variety of names given various honey drinks; Dr. Beck[8] has a good discussion of these. It is obvious that not everyone agrees on the common terminology, but the following names are ones on which most people do agree, and for the most part, these will serve to designate the more common honey concoctions:

mead:	honey wine (honey only and no spices added)
sack mead:	sweet honey wine (but honey only, no sugar)
metheglin:	spiced mead
sack metheglin:	sweet spiced mead
pymeat:	honey-sweetened grape wine
cyser:	mead made with apple juice

---

[8]Beck, Bodog F. 1938. *Honey and Health.* Robert M. McBride and Company, New York. 272 pages.

melomel: mead made with fruit juice other than apple
hippocras: spiced pymeat
hydromel: a weak (watered) mead

The current status of honey drinks

The quality of all alcoholic beverages, perhaps of all foods, has been much improved in the past few decades through research. Not only do we better understand the fermentation and aging processes, but we know enough about pasteurization to prevent the growth of undesirable organisms that might cause off-flavors. The result is that grape wine, which has always ranked high as a beverage, is better today than ever; it offers strong competition to all other alcoholic drinks, whatever their origin.

Still, during one year's search, I found eleven different honey wines in local liquor stores in our small city. (New York State is fairly primitive regarding legislation on alcohol and wines, and they cannot yet be sold in grocery stores.)

The honey wines I found were made in Canada, England, Denmark, Poland, and New York City. Some were good but many were sweet, especially those made for the kosher trade. Several years ago I consulted with one of these companies and found that, according to kosher law, yeast cells do not (cannot) exist, and are not responsible for the fermentation of wine. Therefore, they do not add yeast in making wine. The must is made and put into a barrel with the hope that alcohol will be formed. Often the fermentation is slow and some acetic acid (the acid in vinegar) is made. This results in a wine with a high volatile acid (the acetic acid) and an off-flavor. Adding honey covers up this bad taste. The only recommendation I could make to the company was that they pour some mead nearly finished into a new batch, thus introducing yeast. I elaborated, saying that this would make a more uniform tasting mead, from batch to batch; this is true, and provides an acceptable excuse for what would otherwise be an unacceptable practice. I think the mead from the company in question has improved since, but it is still too sweet.

Honey is used in a wide variety of dessert wines, aperitifs, and after-dinner drinks in many parts of the world. The best known of these are Drambouie, Irish Mist, and Polish Krupnik. I've had some American-made Krupnik, but it did not compare with that made in Poland. Given a choice, I rank Krupnik first, Drambouie and Irish Mist about equal. This is not to suggest that Drambouie or Irish Mist are inferior, for they are not; all three are delicious drinks. They are made using the local whiskey, herbs, and heather honey. Now that it is possible to buy 190 proof[9] alcohol, one may make a good after-dinner drink at home, perhaps using a good mead as a base. Aging, the blending of the herbs, and the type of honey used are all important aspects of the art.

Is there a future for honey drinks? It is limited, I believe. The reasons are simple: the price of honey is high, and there are already many good alcoholic beverages on the market. However, the quality of good honey drinks is as good as the quality of any others and I'm certain they will continue to be made. A good promotion program might well prove my assessment to be pessimistic.

---

[9]High proof alcohol is not available in every state.

II.

Honey

To make mead, one dilutes honey with water, adds nutrients and yeast, and allows the mixture to ferment. Because honey is the chief ingredient, the flavor of the mead depends, to a large extent, on the honey used. But honeys vary greatly; not two are alike. For this reason it is important to discuss what honey is, how it is made, and how it varies, even from hive to hive.

Honey is a natural product. To make honey, bees gather nectar, usually from flowers.[1] Flowers produce nectar, a sweet, sap-like liquid, to attract bees and other insects. As a bee moves from one flower to another, she carries pollen grains entrapped in her hair. Pollen is the male germ cell; when it is deposited on the female part (stigma) of a flower of the same species, it grows and the flower's female parts are fertilized (cross pollinated). Honey bees feed exclusively on pollen and nectar; pollen is their source of protein and nectar their source of carbohydrate. It is not unreasonable to say that nectar is the bee's reward for her work.

Nectar

Each species of flowering plant has a flower with unique color, shape, design, odor, and nectar. There is a sound biological reason for this. It is important that a honey bee fly from a flower of one species to another flower of the same species. Pollen from a white clover flower will fertilize only another white clover flower. No pollen can fertilize another plant species. By having different colors, shapes etc., plants mark themselves so that bees will recognize them.

Several researchers have documented the honey bee's remarkable fidelity to a flower species. Only about seven per cent of honey bees visit more than one species of flower on a single trip to the field. This information was gleaned by examining pollen loads collected by bees. Pollen grains have distinctive sizes, shapes, colors, and designs, and may be identified using a microscope. Many bees not only visit only one flower species on

---

[1]A very small number of plants have extrafloral nectaries, glands not associated with flowers, that produce a sweet sap similar chemically and physically to nectar bees collect from flowers. Cotton is such a plant. Still another raw material for honey is honeydew, a sweet secretion high in gums and resins, produced by aphids. The "forest honey" of Germany and Switzerland is honeydew honey. Over 99 per cent of honey is produced from nectar from floral nectaries; honey from extrafloral nectaries or honeydew is rare.

a single trip — they may spend their entire field life, two to three weeks, working on a single plant species.

Nectar varies in many ways. The water content may be as low as 50 per cent or as high as 90 per cent. This does not affect the flavor of the final honey, but bees can measure the sugar (solids) content of a nectar, and they prefer the richest. Nectar also varies in ash content; this is important to the mead maker because the ash provides essential minerals and other nutrients needed for yeast growth. Some honeys provide more of these growth factors than do others.

The mead maker's primary concern with nectar is its color and flavor. Nectar may be colorless or coal black; some nectars and their resulting honeys are almost flavorless while others are minty or fruity, and sometimes harsh and strong.

Making nectar into honey

Three things are done by bees when nectar is made into honey. First, the moisture content of the nectar is reduced to about 18 per cent. This creates a solution with a high osmotic pressure, which prevents the growth of microorganisms. Reducing the moisture content of the nectar also saves storage space.

A second change in nectar made by bees is the breaking (inversion) of the twelve-carbon sugar, sucrose, into two six-carbon sugars, fructose and glucose. Bees produce an enzyme, invertase, that brings about the change. Sucrose is the chief sugar in nectar; on the average only about one per cent of honey is sucrose.

The third change, one discovered in the 1960's, is the production by the bee of glucose oxidase, and its addition to honey. This enzyme attacks the sugar glucose and produces gluconic acid and hydrogen peroxide. Only a small portion of the glucose in honey is affected. Gluconic acid is the chief acid in honey. Honey is an acid food; it has a relatively low pH, about the same as that of most grape juice, although the total acid content is only one third to one half that found in grape juice. This is because honey is a poorly buffered solution and a small amount of acid or base will move the pH appreciably one way or the other. Thus, while diluted honey is a hospitable medium for wine yeast growth, one must add acid to make a good mead. (Not all mead makers agree on this issue, and it is discussed further below.)

Although it is not important in mead making, the role of hydrogen peroxide is worth discussing further, as it is another factor that makes honey a stable, unusual food. The glucose oxidase enzyme is active and produces gluconic acid and hydrogen peroxide only when the honey is being ripened or is diluted. During this time the honey lacks the high osmotic pressure that protects it at normal moisture levels. The quantity of hydrogen peroxide produced is sufficient to protect the unripe or diluted honey against attack by microbes, but not high enough to have any adverse effect on those (bees or otherwise) who eat it.

Crystallized honey

Honey is a supersaturated sugar solution. As a result, when nuclei on which crystals might form are present, it crystallizes. Beekeepers and honey processors normally heat honey to destroy both the osmophilic yeasts that are present and the nuclei on which crystals might grow. Most honeys will remain liquid on a grocery shelf for four to six months; however, given time, almost any honey will crystallize. This has no adverse effect on the nature or flavor of the honey. The speed with which honeys crystallize depends upon the glucose-fructose ratio, which varies widely. Honeys high in fructose are much slower to crystallize. In making mead it is necessary to liquify any crystallized honey, but this is done automatically when the

1. *This colony is being examined in the early spring. Making mead and keeping bees are similar in that time is needed to produce the final product.*

honey-water mixture is boiled. Boiling and the reasons for doing so are discussed in detail below.

Growth factors in honey

Honey is more than just a sugar solution. It contains many vitamins, minerals, plant pigments, and other materials, which give each honey its distinctive color, flavor, an odor. Many of these materials aid yeasts in their growth; yeasts, like all living things, need a balanced diet and this means more than sugar.

One way of judging the quantity of these substances in a honey is to determine its ash content. This is done by heating a weighed honey sample to 600°C in an oven; what remains is the ash. The ash content of darker honeys is many times higher than that of light honeys.

When honey is diluted to make mead, the growth factors are likewise diluted, and certain factors must be added to speed up the fermentation. Without the addition of these materials, the fermentation is slow, taking many months. The chief reason for forcing a fast fermentation is to raise the alcoholic content quickly so that the alcohol will protect the resulting product; alcohol is itself a good preservative.

Pollen in honey

Pollen is a natural contaminant in honey. Varietal honeys may be identified by the pollen they contain. The quantity of pollen present in a honey varies with its origin; some plants produce far more pollen than others. Two notable examples of "yellow honey," made so by the large quantity of pollen present, are those made from dandelion and from Brazilian pepper (sometimes called Mexican pepper). Although pollen has a somewhat bitter taste, the quantity present in most honey is too little for it to have any adverse effect on the flavor. Pollen is mostly protein, but contains a very small amount of fat. I've seen the addition of pollen recommended in mead making, but I don't think it is necessary or advisable. That pollen that is naturally present in honey adds to the nutrients present and aids in yeast growth.

The effect of filtration on honey

Some honey packers filter their honey, a practice most beekeepers reject. Filtration removes crystal nuclei, while heating destroys them; the two processes coupled will do much to increase the shelf life of liquid honey and this is why they are done. However, filtration removes pollen and thus certain of the natural factors present in honey. If filtration and heating are done carefully, most of the honey flavor is retained. For the best results in mead making, the honey should not be filtered.

Comb and brood in mead making

On rare occasion I have seen mead recipes that suggest that adding comb and anything it might contain, including brood, might improve the mead. I've tried the concoction, although I had a strong objection to drinking it; neither the flavor nor the fermentation was improved. It is not a process I would recommend. Still, primitive people who make honey wine and beer do so and apparently relish the idea. It is highly probable that many English, Polish, and Nordic mead makers of earlier times did the same, though some of the early English literature does advise that only clean, pure honey be used in mead making.

I have observed the process of East African beer making; it often involves adding everything and anything to the mixture to be fermented. In the normal process of harvesting honey, the log hives are smoked and the bees driven from one end. The beekeeper then scoops out about half of the hive's contents, hoping that the majority will be honey. Sometimes the honey and wax are separated, but often what is collected is mashed in preparation for the fermentation. It may include some live bees as well as cells of brood, pollen, and honey. Water and grain are added. The mixture is fermented for about three days, by which time it reaches five to six percent alcohol and is ready to be consumed. I visited with one beekeeper in Africa who purchased the dregs from the fermentation barrels and placed them in a solar wax extractor. He recovered sufficient beeswax to make it a paying proposition.

Cappings honey

Cappings, the wax coverings of cells of honey that are removed with a knife when one is extracting, contain honey that is difficult to remove without melting the wax and destroying the flavor of the honey in the process. It is possible to soak cappings in cold or slightly warm (100-110°F) water and to remove the honey. The cappings may then be rendered in the normal manner and the honey used to make mead. This is an instance where a hydrometer, an instrument that measures the sugar content of a liquid, is helpful to measure the amount of honey in the honey-water mixture so that honey or water may be added to yield the right proportions.

A word of warning! Cappings-melter honey is that which has been separated from cappings with a Brand melter or some other heating device. It is not fit for any purpose, in my opinion, especially mead making. I have long advised beekeepers against the use of Brand melters, but without much success. The wax product they make is excellent, but any honey from a Brand melter has a burned flavor and is darkened an average of about 15 points on the Pfund grader, an instrument for measuring honey color.

The effect of diluting honey

In making mead, water is added so that the final mixture contains about 22 per cent (rather than the 82 per cent in honey) solids, most of which is sugar. Adding water to honey dilutes the color, flavor, and nutrients. It is for this reason that stronger honeys often make the best mead. Honeys that are too strong for table use often make an excellent mead, and mild honeys may produce meads that are too bland. The dilution of the nutrients in honey causes changes too, and may, especially in the case of the lighter honeys, leave too little of the needed nutrients for the yeast cells to flourish. The dilution of the nutrients is compensated for by adding fruit juices or chemicals. Adding acid stabilizes the mixture.

The special keeping quality of honey

Honey is an unusual agricultural product. It may be stored for a year or more, and if not exposed to too high temperatures, will retain much of its flavor and quality.

Stories that honey retains its quality indefinitely are not correct. I have had several samples of both liquid and comb honey that were 25 to 75 years old. These honeys are always black and their taste is unappealing, whatever their origin. There is a slow but definite deterioration of old honey; this is speeded up by high temperatures and sunlight. While large quantities of honey have been stored successfully in unheated warehouses for one to three years, we have found it best to freeze samples that are to be retained for a year or more for class use. We have kept comb honey and liquid honey in glass in this manner for several years with no detectable change in the character of the honey.

III.

Equipment for Mead Making

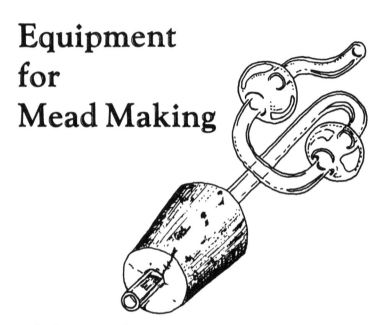

Ideally one would have a separate room (or cellar) in which to conduct the fermentations, make the necessary chemical tests, and store bottles for aging. However, what is ideal and what is realistic are quite often altogether different. It is therefore best to talk about what most expert mead and wine makers consider reasonable and safe conditions.

Temperature control and the ideal temperature for yeast growth is discussed elsewhere; the chief concern here is to emphasize that a temperature of about 65° to 68°F. (18 to 19°C) is to be desired for both the fermentation and storage of mead. If there is a choice between a slightly cooler or warmer room, the former is the better choice. At the same time, and perhaps more important, one should not allow great fluctuations in temperature, for this can be far more harmful. Sunlight, too, should be excluded from the mead room, because it can cause temperature fluctuations and encourage the growth of some undesirable organisms.

Sanitation is discussed in greater length below. Spores of molds, fungi, yeasts, and other microbes float free in the air, and while they don't actively seek places to grow, they are nevertheless always present and able to germinate given the opportunity. Being able to minimize dust is therefore important. Every time a barrel, carboy, or bottle is opened, there is a risk of contamination.

It is helpful if the bench on which the analyses are conducted is made of stone, porcelain, stainless steel, or some other substance that may be washed with disinfectant to eliminate undesirable organisms in the immediate vicinity.

Sanitation

Yeast cells will grow in a wide range of mediums. It is obvious that what is attractive for a yeast cell will also be attractive to a number of different bacteria and other microorganisms. Sulfur dioxide, properly used, gives the mead maker a great deal of protection since yeast cells will grow without difficulty in low concentrations of sulfur dioxide, while many of the undesirable creatures that may infect the wine will not. However, sulfur dioxide is no substitute for sanitation. The proper use of sulfur dioxide is discussed in chapter IV.

Clorox, the commercial bleach, is an excellent product to sterilize certain types of wine-making equipment. *Clorox* contains sodium hypochlorite, which releases chlorine into a water solution. Chlorine has been used since shortly after 1900 to purify water; very low concentrations will kill a wide range of microorganisms. In low concentration the chlorine is not toxic to man, though the taste of chlorinated water is usually repulsive. Chlorine is highly toxic to yeasts, and if accidentally introduced into a fermentation container, and not thoroughly removed, it may prevent or stop a fermentation.

Clorox should not be used to clean wooden barrels or other wooden implements. It is an excellent product to clean glassware, including carboys and jugs, but these must be thoroughly rinsed to remove all the remaining chlorine before they are used to make mead. In the home laboratory, a weak solution of *Clorox* may be used to wipe the laboratory bench clean before inoculations are made. Again, if the home laboratory becomes a source of infection because of dampness or spillage, a commercial chlorine solution may be used to rescue the situation.

It is dangerous to use soap and detergents in cleaning winemaking equipment. It is too easy to leave a soap residue or film that may adversely affect the flavor of the wine in the container. Certainly one needs soap to clean a glass jug, and this is satisfactory if the soap is flushed away with large volumes of water when the cleaning is done.

Washing soda (sodium carbonate or soda ash) is used widely in wineries as a cleaning solution, even for barrels, though this is probably not the best of practices. So long as the washing soda is flushed away it will cause no harm. Most wine supply shops will stock a supply of washing soda.

Storing barrels poses a special problem for the home wine maker. To keep a barrel in good condition it should be stored full of water. If a barrel dries, it is extremely difficult, and oftentimes impossible, to force it to swell properly and not leak. It is important to clean a barrel immediately after a fermentation and to remove the dead yeast cells before it is filled with water for storage. Sulfur dioxide tablets or powders may be added to the water periodically as insurance against contamination. Sulfur candles are recommended for giving a barrel a final cleaning before a must is added for a fermentation.

One reasonably satisfactory method of cleaning and sterilizing barrels is to steam them with a constant jet of steam for fifteen to twenty minutes. The steam will do no harm to an already soaked and wet barrel. However, steam is not always available.

Barrels, carboys and jugs

Not too many years ago, most wine was fermented and underwent its first aging in wooden casks. These were usually made of oak, the white oak from the northern United States being preferred, even by Europeans. Redwood has been used satisfactorily on the west coast. The casks, kegs, barrels, or whatever they might be called, and there are a great variety of names, were reused year after year. Just before a new wine was placed in an old barrel it was "sulfited" by burning a sulfur candle in it; this was usually a satisfactory method of sterilizing the barrel.

2. This barrel is being flushed with water prior to being filled. Great care must be taken to clean barrels thoroughly. Photo by Paul Comer.

3. A functional mead maker's cellar. The barrels are mounted on racks to save space. Note pads are kept with each barrel to record what has taken place. Photo by Paul Comer.

New barrels pose a problem for the mead or wine maker, for the mead will pick up a great deal of flavor from new oak wood. Many home wine makers purchase used whiskey barrels from which much of the oak flavor has been extracted (the flavor of whiskey is in large part that extracted from the oak).

Even charred barrels produce an oak flavor; charring is usually done so that the charcoal will help in the removal of harsh flavors from the wine. As a barrel is reused year after year, the wood has less and less effect on the flavor of the mead it contains. Further, the wood takes on certain characteristics from the mead, so the same type of mead should be made in the same barrel year after year. The mead maker just starting to practice the art must be aware of these problems. One just cannot purchase an old wine barrel with the desired background; perhaps this is sufficient reason to use some other type of container.

Some barrels, especially the smaller ones, are coated on the inside with paraffin. This practice negates the use of wood which has the advantage of breathing, and makes the use of such a barrel not unlike using a glass carboy. However, coating with paraffin is probably necessary for smaller barrels, the ones that hold 25 gallons or less. Small barrels (5, 10, or 25 gallons) absorb oxygen too fast, and wines stored in them for long periods of time have an overoxidized taste.

Glass is now the preferred container in which to make mead at home. The reasons appear to be twofold. First, one may follow the course of the fermentation with ease. Second, it is easier to clean and store a glass carboy or jug than a wooden barrel. The five gallon size is most popular.

Some wine is being fermented, and often stored, in plastic containers. Such containers are sold in some shops that cater to the home wine-making trade. I suggest plastic be avoided, as it may sometimes produce off-flavors. Time may prove this suggestion invalid, but in wine making it is usually best to be cautious and to take the known and proven pathways.

The fullness of the fermenter or fermentation container and the use of antifoams are discussed below.

Fermentation valves

Sanitation is mentioned repeatedly in books and articles on wine making. This is because it is easy to introduce a foreign microbe into the fermenting wine. Fermentation valves are designed to protect the wine. Properly fitting fermentation valves should be part of every wine maker's sanitation scheme.

It is only fair to point out that a fermentation valve, as such, is really not necessary. A plug of cotton in a carboy neck or barrel bung will serve the purpose. If cotton is used it should be of the sterilized type; alternatively, one may touch a match to the cotton wad, push it into place while still burning, then blow out or cover the remaining flame with a fireproof object to extinguish the flame. Cotton will serve to entrap and prevent the entrance of foreign bacteria into a mead or wine just as will a water-type fermentation valve.

The advantage of a fermentation valve with water is that one can better follow the course of the fermentation and see what is happening. The first sign of escaping carbon dioxide bubbling through the water gives assurance that the fermentation has started; then, the end of the fermentation is clearly visible as the bubbling will stop.

Before the fermentation valve or cotton wad is put into place, that part of the inside of the carboy neck or the barrel bung touched by the valve or cotton should be washed and wiped clean and dry. If this is not done a pathway for the entrance of deleterious bacteria might be formed between the cork on the valve (or the cotton) and the container. While sulfur dioxide can protect the fermenting wine from infection, this should not be relied upon alone, nor should sulfur dioxide be considered a substitute for good sanitary practices.

4. *Two types of fermentation valves. Both of these models have the advantage that liquid cannot be sucked back into the carboy. A fermentation valve allows the carbon dioxide to escape without permitting microbes to enter the fermentation vessel.*

5. *A homemade fermentaton valve made with a piece of bent glass and a test tube. A fermentation valve allows the mead maker to follow the course of the fermentation by watching the rate at which carbon dioxide escapes.*

Several types of fermentation valves are available, and it is also possible to make fermentation valves at home with a piece of glass, rubber tubing, cork, and a jar or test tube. The best valves are made so that the water in the valve cannot enter the fermentation container if a back pressure develops. Although escaping carbon dioxide usually keeps pressure on the water valve, and the flow of gas usually is from the inside to the outside, a change in temperature may reverse this gas movement for a brief period of time, sucking the contents of the water fermentation valve back into the newly fermenting mead. Either a cork or rubber stopper may be used to fit around the fermentation valve and to close the barrel bung or carboy opening. Adding a pinch of chemical that will release sulfur dioxide into the water in the fermentation valve is probably advisable. Very occasionally, especially during a violent fermentation, if the container is too full, some of the mead may escape into the fermentation valve, where mold or bacteria will develop in it. A small amount of sulfur dioxide will prevent this. If such a condition develops, the fermentation valve should be replaced as soon as the problem is noted; adding sulfur dioxide gives only interim protection.

Temperature control

An ideal fermentation and mead storage room is dark and has a uniform temperature throughout the year. It is because it is easier to control the temperature in a cave or cellar that these have been used traditionally for wine making. They are also cooler in summer than the average above-ground structure, again increasing their value to the wine-maker. A cellar or cave has the added advantage of being dark. A major disadvantage is that cellars and caves may be damp, giving rise to mold growth over the containers and often an undesirable odor.

There is no reason why almost any room in a modern home cannot be remade into a wine cellar. In fact, a dry room may have some advantages over a damp cellar. As already mentioned, the ideal temperature for a wine cellar is 65 to 68°F. (18 to 19°C.). Cellars in which the temperature sometimes falls lower will pose little problem. It must be remembered that below 50°F. (10°C.), an active fermentation may cease because it is too cool for the yeast cells to grow (see Stuck wines), but the lower temperatures merely slow the aging process. One must be wary of cellars in which the temperature fluctuates too much. A rapid rise in temperature may cause corks in bottles to move or cause wine to escape through loose corks.

While temperatures lower than 68°F. (19°C.) cause little harm, high temperatures, especially in excess of 75 or 80°F. (24 to 26°C.), can be detrimental, especially during aging. The major danger is that off-flavors may be caused by too rapid aging or overoxidation. Undesirable color changes may also take place in wines stored at high temperatures. Temperatures over 85°F. (29°C.) may kill the yeasts in an active fermentation.

The fermentation process is exothermic, that is, heat is given off as yeast cells feed, grow, and divide. This occurs only when there is an active fermentation in progress. Heat production is not a problem if wine is being made in containers that hold 50 gallons or less. When a 100-gallon barrel is used, a slight rise in the temperature of the must may be noted during the active fermentation. Commercial wineries find this excess heat production a serious problem in their large fermentation vats. They sometimes control it by pumping the fermenting wine through a heat exchanger. In a heat exchanger the warmer wine passing on one side of a stainless steel plate is cooled by flowing cold water on the other side. In very large active fermentation vats the temperature is often in the 80's (27 to 32°C.); however, at this higher temperature the fermentation proceeds more rapidly which is considered advantageous by some. The question is debatable.

IV.

Yeasts
and the
Fermentation

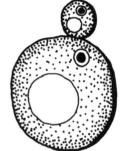
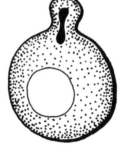
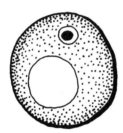

In the first chapter it was explained that yeast cells are living organisms. As they grow and consume food, a variety of products are formed. The two most common are carbon dioxide and alcohol. This is not done purposefully, or because either is of any value to the growing cell; it is merely a result of the inefficient metabolism of the yeast cells. They cannot do otherwise.

In this chapter we are concerned with how we can force a population of yeast cells to make alcohol most efficiently and to our advantage. Besides alcohol and carbon dioxide, yeast cells manufacture a variety of products, some of which can impart bad flavors or have adverse effects on the aging, stability, and physical appearance of the final product. Bread yeast, for example, can be used to ferment a wide variety of juices and musts, but the resulting product, whatever its origin, will have an undesirable bready flavor.

All ripe fruits have yeast cells (so-called wild yeasts) growing on their surfaces, and these may be used for the fermentation. Those experienced in wine making agree that, while the occasional wild yeast may give a good, or rarely even a superior flavor, the careful wine maker relies exclusively on cultures of known yeasts introduced into the aqueous solution in quantities sufficient to overwhelm the growth of any other yeasts present. The yeasts used in commercial wine making have been selected from their wild relatives.

The best yeast for mead

Stating which type of yeast makes the best mead is dangerous. Many factors influence the character and taste of a wine or mead, and among these is the strain of yeast used. Yeasts vary in the speed at which they grow and the flavor they impart, among other characteristics.

The yeasts used to make sauterne-type wines generally are good for mead making; in fact, most yeasts suggested for making a white wine will serve equally well. Many mead makers prefer champagne-type yeasts because their greater agglutinating power is thought to aid in clearing the mead. Most champagne-type yeasts form a product with a good flavor. I have seen advertisements for special yeasts for mead making, but none of those I have tested has had any special virtues over good white wine yeasts.

Yeast cells

The world of microbes may be divided into four groups: bacteria, fungi, protozoa, and algae. Yeasts belong to the fungi, and when the fungi are subdivided, the yeasts are grouped with the higher fungi.

The yeasts that are used for fermenting, whether to make bread, beer, wine or whiskey, all belong to the same species, *Saccharomyces cerviseae*. There are obviously many races or subgroups; bacteriologists prefer to use the term strain. Wine yeasts are called *Saccharomyces cerviseae* variety *ellipsoideus*, while those used for other purposes are given other varietal names. In reading the literature on the subject of names and naming, one is struck by the fact that there is much disagreement among the authorities on the subject. Yeast cell taxonomy is not perfect!

In making wine, the use of controlled cultures is to be preferred over the use of the wild yeasts. However, the use of mixed cultures of yeast strains may be of benefit under some circumstances and is just now beginning to receive the attention it deserves.

Yeasts are one-cell organisms. There are no sexes. They multiply by a process called budding; a yeast cell grows and divides into two cells, and these grow some more and again divide.

Under normal circumstances yeasts ferment the sugar glucose more rapidly than they do the sweeter sugar fructose. Honeys vary greatly in their glucose-fructose ratios; those that granulate rapidly are higher in glucose and beekeepers use this fact as a general guide to the glucose-fructose ratio. The chief point here is that a wine with residual sugar content of one per cent may taste much sweeter if most of that sugar is fructose. At the present time, knowledge of this fact is of general interest only; however, as we increase our understanding of yeast strains and their ability to ferment various musts, there will no doubt be an effort to select and control those yeasts that select glucose over fructose.

The ecology of yeast cell growth

The growth of yeast cells introduced into a new must follows a pattern that is typical of the growth of many microorganisms in new media. There is first the "lag phase," during which the total number of cells present changes little. While some cells grow and divide immediately, many die from the shock of their new environment. The lag period may last only hours or it may take days. The wine maker seeks to give the yeast cells the optimum climate in which to grow and, at the same time, to select yeasts that will grow rapidly when presented with new circumstances. The lag period can be a dangerous time, as undesirable microorganisms may also grow and multiply before they are overtaken by the increasing alcoholic content of the new wine or the sheer number of yeast cells.

In the second phase there is rapid growth and multiplication of the cells as they adjust to the medium. This growth continues until it is slowed, and eventually halted, by some limiting factor, the most common of which it too little sugar or too much alcohol. However, several other factors may enter the picture. These include the sugar concentration, degree of acidity (expressed as pH), temperature, lack of nutrients, etc.

The amount of acid in a wine and the pH of the wine are not the same, but they are closely tied together and a proper balance of both is of the utmost importance in wine making. The acid content of a wine has an especially strong bearing on its flavor, while the correct pH is necessary for proper yeast growth.

The acid content of the wine is concerned with the amount of acid in the wine. The pH of a wine is described as its "active acidity." The pH scale has been designed for our convenience and to tell in exact terms what the acid in a wine is doing. A pH of 7 means that a solution is neutral. A material with a pH lower than 7 is acid, while one that has a pH higher than 7 is basic.

Grape juice, in fact most fruit juices and wines, are acid solutions. They have a pH in the range of 3 to 4, sometimes slightly higher, rarely lower. However, it is important to understand that solutions with equal pH's do not have equal amounts of acid. Grape juice and honey are two natural products that illustrate this point. The pH of both is about the same, that is, about 3 to 4; however, the total acid content of grape juice is two to four times that of honey. It is very easy to change the pH of honey because there is little else in solution to modify or control it. A small amount of acid or a small amount of base added to honey will change the pH considerably. This must be kept in mind when honey wine (mead) is made. The same is not true of grape juice, as the many other materials in solution help to control the pH and modify any fluctuations in it. The problem comes to the forefront when sugar wines are made. It is important that nutrients, and the most common additive is ammonium phosphate, be balanced with the right amount of acid. Ammonium phosphate causes a solution to be more basic. Fortunately, there are relatively simple methods for testing pH (described in chapter X).

Yeast starters and their propagation

From the foregoing discussion it is clear that the best wines and meads will be made by using a fresh, massive inoculation of actively growing yeast cells. The commercial winery has the advantage of a laboratory where cultures may be maintained and grown at will. The home wine maker must content himself with what is available. Yeasts are generally sold on agar slants, in test tubes stoppered with cotton, or in a dried form. The prejudice against the use of dried yeasts has been overcome in recent years.

To propagate the yeast culture, one starts with a small volume and increases it gradually. This is true of a dried yeast culture, too, even though the directions on the packet may indicate the yeast may be introduced directly. When an agar slant is available, one may add sterile must to the test tube; however, if must works its way under the agar, carbon dioxide may force it to move up the test tube and to contact and wet the cotton plug. The best technique is to obtain a bacteriological loup (which has a diameter of slightly less than a quarter inch), make it red hot in the flame from a gas cook stove, insert the red-hot loop into the test tube containing agar, and transfer a loup-full of yeast to sterile must in a second test tube. The second test tube should be sterilized and stoppered with cotton. Of course, the hot loup will kill the first yeast cells it contacts, so the loup must be moved along the growing yeast culture until it is cooled. The test tube into which the culture is transferred usually contains only a few milliliters or a tablespoonful of must. When this is fermenting strongly, which will occur in about two days, it is poured into a small flask containing about a cup of sterile must, again with a cotton stopper. This in turn is used to inoculate, in succession, a gallon, five gallons, 50 gallons, etc. On a percentage basis, one may use as little as one per cent or as much as five per cent inoculum.

The small batches of must used in the initial stages of building a culture may be made sterile by being brought to a boil. An alternative is to use small cans of cider or grape juice; those packaged as single servings are adequate for the first two steps. This amount of juice would have little effect on the final mead; perhaps apple juice is to be preferred. Needless to say, once a must is sterilized for use in this manner, or a can of fruit juice opened, it should be used immediately (when cooled), because a must that stands, even if exposed to the air only briefly, will be quickly contaminated by air-borne microbes. One never prevents all undesirable microbes from entering a new must, but the aim is to build a culture that will outnumber and overwhelm the unwanted ones.

Dried yeast cultures

The most common variety of yeast available for mead making is dried yeast sold in a sealed foil. Not everyone has had success in using dried yeasts, and a better understanding of how they should be used can be gained from understanding how they are prepared for market.

The process of preparing the dried yeasts is called lyophilization; it is also called freeze-drying. The cells are frozen and placed under vacuum until the water is removed. In this dried state many of the yeast cells will remain alive and healthy for years at room temperature, but it is best to keep dried yeasts in a refrigerator or frozen. If they are subjected to high temperatures, or worse, fluctuating temperatures, some will be killed.

During the freeze-drying process many of the cells are killed and others are injured, perhaps as many as 80 to 95 per cent. The injured cells can repair themselves if they are placed in a favorable growing medium. It is not unreasonable to understand that putting dried yeasts into a liquid, even though it be one they normally prefer, can be a shock. If the medium is especially high in acid, has a low pH, or, worse, an abundance of free sulfur dioxide, the shock may be so great that all of the yeast cells die. When a dried yeast culture fails it is usually for one of these reasons. Misuse of sulfur dioxide is the most common problem and is stressed elsewhere. Twelve to 24 hours should be allowed to pass before adding yeast to a newly sulfured must.

A technique I prefer for starting a culture of new yeast cells is to introduce the yeast culture into some apple juice kept in a small flask. The six-ounce cans of apple juice, intended for an individual serving, are just right for starting a culture. The canned apple juice is sterile and free of any microbes that could have a bad effect on the mead. The ideal flask has a volume of 250 or 500 ml; these are usually available in drug stores. The flask should be boiled in water for 15 minutes, then allowed to dry and cool for about five minutes before the apple juice is poured in. One should add only enough juice so the flask is one quarter to one third full. One must use a funnel or be very careful to pour the juice in in such a way that none comes into contact with the inside of the neck of the flask. If it does, one should start over, as even a small amount of juice in the inside neck could form a route by which undesirable yeasts and molds could enter. The apple juice should be at room temperature. The yeast is poured into the juice and the flask loosely stoppered with a cotton plug. Sterile household-type cotton will prevent undesirable microbes from entering. After about 48 to 72 hours, the medium should show the signs of an active fermentation. Swirling the flask gently will cause perhaps as much as half an inch of foam to form, as carbon dioxide rises to the top. The reason for having the flask only about one quarter to one third full is now apparent, for with violent fermentation so much foam would be formed that it would wet the cotton. When the new culture shows signs of a strong fermentation, it may be used to start a larger batch of wine or mead. Ideally, the culture should make up five per cent of the volume to which it is added. One may add the contents of a small flask to the mead must in a gallon jug, and then use the contents of the jug to start a larger carboy or barrel.

The osmophilic yeasts

The osmophilic yeasts are so called because they live in solutions that have a high osmotic pressure, such as honey. In fact, they cannot survive (or at least grow and reproduce themselves) in solutions containing less than about 30 per cent sugar. In other respects they are similar and closely related to the yeasts used to make mead and wine.

As a group of living organisms, the osmophilic yeasts have received relatively little study. How they are spread and survive year to year is not known. We believe that yeast cells are picked up in nectar gathered by bees; in addition, some probably survive throughout the year in the bee hive.

Just as the osmophilic yeasts cannot grow in a honey solution that is too dilute, so their growth is also stopped when the water concentration of the honey is reduced below about 19 per cent. Thus, in normal honey stored in the hive, they remain in a resting stage until an environment develops that enables them to grow and reproduce.

Honey is hygroscopic. This it, because of its high sugar concentration, it will pick up water on its surface. It is possible for honey in an open container to pick up sufficient water in the very top surface for a fermentation to take place. Tons of honey have been lost through fermentations caused by the osmophilic yeasts. They can produce sufficient carbon dioxide to burst the containers in which the honey is stored. It is because of this danger that most honey on the market is pasteurized.

Osmophilic yeasts are of no value in mead making. They produce too little alcohol, and what they do produce is of poor flavor. Raw honey (unpasteurized) may be used to make mead (though, as I indicated elsewhere, I prefer not to do so) and the osmophilic yeasts will not interfere with the fermentation, because the honey is diluted past the point at which they can grow.

Attempting to salvage honey that has been fermented (even partially) by osmophilic yeasts and using it to make mead is likewise not advisable. However, I need not belabor this point, as the foul odor created by osmophilic yeasts is usually sufficient warning. The fermentation of honey is a plague to beekeepers and once it occurs they usually learn to take precautions against it happening again. Fermented honey may be fed to the bees, though it has never been clear to me whether they make use of all of it or discard portions.

Sulfur and sulfiting wines

Sulfur dioxide is a bactericidal and fungicidal agent widely used in the food industry. It is used to preserve fruit juices, jellies, and preserves. It has a very special application in the wine industry. Every home wine maker should be familiar with how and why it, is used.

Sulfur dioxide in the amount of about 50 parts per million (50 p.p.m.) will prevent the growth of most of the micro-organisms that might adversely affect or destroy a wine, either during or after fermentation. Wine yeasts are not affected by this much sulfur dioxide and the fermentation proceeds normally with it present. However, too much sulfur dioxide, more than 60 to 70 p.p.m., will usually inhibit yeast growth. Sulfur dioxide has the added advantage of preventing overoxidation of wine, thus protecting its delicate color and flavor. There is only one precaution in the use of sulfur dioxide: when it is added to a new must, the solution should be allowed to stand for several hours before the yeast starter is added. If this is not done, the yeast may be killed.

When first added to a mead, sulfur dioxide gives it an unpleasant flavor. As the sulfur dioxide breaks down, this taste disappears, as does the sulfur dioxide itself. Sulfur dioxide appears to have no effects that would indicate that it should not be used either at home or commercially.

Tablets containing potassium metabisulfite or, less commonly, sodium bisulfite, may be purchased from wine supply shops. The normal tablets used at the rate of one per gallon are calibrated to liberate 50 p.p.m. of sulfur dioxide per gallon of must. These chemicals may also be purchased as powders, sometimes preweighed for immediate use. One gram of potassium metabisulfite will produce 150 p.p.m. of sulfur dioxide per gallon while one gram of sodium bisulfite liberates 160 p.p.m. per gallon. The tablets and powders are reasonably stable and may be kept for a year or more at room temperature without losing their effectiveness. They must be stored where they can be kept dry.

Meads should be sulfited two or three times during their manufacture, each time at about the same level or raising the sulfur dioxide content to the same level. Freshly diluted honey should be sulfited immediately at the rate of 50 p.p.m. If the honey-water mixture is boiled, the sulfur dioxide is added after it has cooled. Under average conditions, 25 p.p.m. or half of the original amount will be left after two months, which may be the time of the first or second racking. All, or almost all, of the sulfur dioxide will be gone at the end of four or five months. Each time the wine is racked the sulfur dioxide content should be increased to 50 or 60 p.p.m. The last dose of sulfur dioxide is given when the mead is bottled. Methods for measuring the amount of sulfur dioxide present in a wine are somewhat complex and require equipment not usually available to home wine makers. More important, the breakdown times cited above are such as to encourage a very slight overdose. This is one instance in biology where a slight overdose will do no harm.

Most of the tablets that release sulfur dioxide are slow to dissolve. They may be ground up with a small amount of wine in a teacup and added to the new mead. However, it is easier to add the tablets to the jug or barrel several hours or a day before bottling. It is only necessary to stir the honey-water gently before bottling to insure uniform distribution of the sulfur dioxide throughout.

Antifoams

Antifoams are widely used in the food industry. They have some application in the wine industry and under certain circumstances may be helpful to the home mead maker. One would not use an antifoam that might contaminate a home-

6. In addition to adding antifoam to the must, one may use his finger to wipe a ring of antifoam around the inside of the carboy. The bubbles of escaping carbon dioxide break when they hit the antifoam. Photo by E. S. Phillips.

7. Without antifoam it is necessary to leave a headspace to accommodate the active fermentation. Dry, clean cotton may be substituted for a fermentation valve as has been done here but has the disadvantage that one cannot follow the course of the fermentation so easily. Photo by E. S. Phillips.

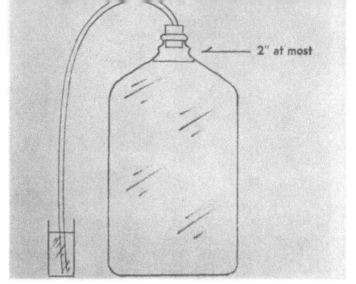

2" at most

8. The carboy may be nearly filled if antifoam is used. A different type of fermentation valve is illustrated here. Photo by E. S. Phillips.

made honey beer where a head is wanted, but since heads are not wanted with meads, their use is no problem.

Silicon, the commonest element, making up over 28 per cent of the earth, is the basis for antifoams. In combination with oxygen, silicon prevents the formation of foam. Antifoams are non-toxic, leave no aftertaste, and have no undesirable characteristics that make their use questionable.

If several drops of an antifoam[1] are added to a five-gallon carboy of fermenting mead, the carboy may be filled to the very top of its shoulder, leaving only about an inch and a half or two inches under the cork in the fermentation valve. Thus, the headspace in the carboy is very small and there is less danger of contamination. The lack of a large headspace makes storage of a mead easier; it also aids when one is transporting a freshly pressed juice that may start to ferment before it reaches its final destination. Most of the home wine-makers' shops stock antifoams and their use should be investigated; most will be pleased with the results.

[1]There are many types of antifoams made for different purposes. The precise quantity to use is usually indicated on the bottle.

V.
Recipes and Formulas

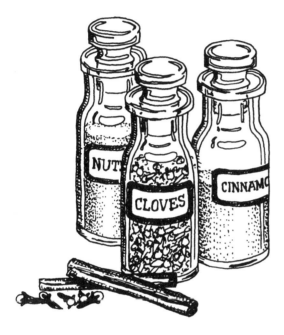

As explained, yeast cells cannot live on sugar alone; they must have a balanced diet. The first serious efforts to make up for the deficiency in nutrients that occurs when honey is diluted with water were made in the 1920's. In an article in *Fruit Products Journal* in 1928 it was suggested that honey could be used to make a good vinegar.[1] Prohibition was still the law, but since wine making is part of the vinegar-making process, a

---

[1] To make vinegar one first conducts a normal fermentation and produces alcohol. After the alcohol is formed, the mother of vinegar is introduced. This bacteria attacks the alcohol and converts it to acetic acid. The alcoholic fermentation is conducted in the absence of oxygen, but the manufacture of alcohol into acetic acid requires oxygen.

knowledgeable reader was presumably able to convert the information for the formulas given so that he might make wine. The author suggested the addition of two ounces each of potassium tartrate and ammonium phosphate for each 30 gallons of water used. The same author, writing in the same journal in 1935, in the post-prohibition era, was more explicit and gave better directions, again suggesting the above additives for making honey wine.

Further directions for making mead appeared in *American Bee Journal* in the same year.[2] It was then recognized that not only was yeast food necessary, but that the addition of acid would enhance the flavor of the final product. Two and a half ounces each of ammonium phosphate and potassium-di-hydrogen phosphate and five ounces of citric acid crystals were added for each ten gallons of diluted honey.

People writing on mead making in the 1930's also recognized that clarification was a very serious problem in mead manufacture. The protein present in honey precipitates over a long period of time, making the final product cloudy. One author suggested the honey-water mixture might be boiled for ten minutes, but he wrote that this was for the purpose of pasteurizing the honey-water mixture; it is not clear if he understood that this aided in the clarification of the final product.

Mead

The mead recipe I have followed for many years is as follows:
>3½ pounds of honey
>1 gallon of water
>4 grams ammonium phosphate
>4 grams urea
>4 grams cream of tartar
>4 grams of a mixture of tartaric and citric acids

---

[2]Filippelo, F., G. L. Marsh and W. V. Cruess. 1935. Suggested directions for making honey mead. American Bee Journal 75: 437-438.

My favorite honey for mead is goldenrod, a honey too strong for table use, but giving a distinctive, pleasant taste when diluted for mead. The water should be unchlorinated spring or well water. A mixture of acids is preferred over using a single one and will improve the final taste slightly. A 1:1 mixture is best; one may also add some malic acid. The final product will be sweet. The use of this basic formula will tell the mead maker if he should add more or less honey and more or less acid. The urea may be the most diffcult item to find in a drug store and its use is not absolutely necessary. If it is not used, the amount of ammonium phosphate used should be increased accordingly. I suggest it would be best to select a champagne-type yeast; variations in yeast types may also be made later.

The honey-water mixture should be boiled for ten to twenty minutes; this will cause the protein in the honey to precipitate and give a final product that is clear. When the mixture is nearly cooled, the nutrients and acid are added. I find it best to pour off a small measure of the must and to dissolve the additives in it. While it is still warm, the mixture is poured into a carboy and a fermentation valve put into place. If a water valve is used it must be of the type that will not suck the water back into the carboy as the mixture cools.

I prefer to add three to four drops of food-type antifoam to the must, thus allowing me to fill the carboy to within about two inches of the cork (very top of the carboy). One must leave sufficient space to add the yeast.

As soon as the must reaches room temperature, the yeast culture is added. If I have a strong yeast culture I feel adding sulfur dioxide at this stage is not necessary. While it is true that undesirable microbes may enter the must while it is cooling, the growth of any such should be overcome by the introduced yeast culture. However, if one adds sulphur dioxide, it is important to delay adding the yeast for 12 to 24 hours after the sulfur dioxide has been mixed in thoroughly.

The fermentation should be complete within three weeks, perhaps sooner, at which time the first decanting and addition of sulfur dioxide should take place. About six months later, after two more decantings, the mead should be ready to bottle. During this preliminary settling and aging the carboys should be kept full by adding mead from a second carboy or jug, or by adding marbles.

Brother Adam's Mead

Some of the best mead I have ever had was that made by Brother Adam, the famous beekeeper of Buckfast Abbey in Southern England. His methods are quite different from my own and were outlined by him in an article in *Bee World* in 1953. Brother Adam rejects many of our modern notions about conducting the fermentation rapidly so as to avoid contamination. He believes too that one can make a good mead in large quantities and in a barrel only. I can argue at length why all this is not correct, but I cannot argue with the final product he produces; his champagne is especially good. The article he has written is worth reading so as to understand the philosophy that underlies his mead making.

The following is a condensed version of Brother Adam's rules: Use soft water (rain or distilled water), a mild-flavored honey (such as clover) is best, a pure yeast culture (Maury, Madeira, or Malaga) is preferred, boil the honey-water mixture (but for one to two minutes only), take great care in sterilizing the fermentation vats, use no chemicals except perhaps a small amount of citric acid when a dry mead is preferred, undertake the fermentation at a low temperature (65 to 70°F.; 16 to 18°C.), summer is the best time for making mead and fall is best for making a sparkling mead (however, in Brother Adam's part of the world summer is not very warm), use oak casks and age the mead (in the casks) a full seven years before it is put into a bottle. I know of no one who advises aging so long, but I do prefer my own mead after it has aged for five or six years.

Brother Adam uses less honey than most and the final alcoholic content of his meads is in the vicinity of eight or nine per cent. It is interesting that in recent years I have increasingly heard comments to the effect that the best flavor in many grape wines may come about when the alcoholic content is lower.

Several spices are mentioned in Brother Adam's article, though he uses spices infrequently. He states that so far as he is concerned only cloves and cinnamon mix well with mead. The grated peel of a lemon added to a barrel of must may improve the flavor of certain meads. If any of these are used, they are added after the honey-water is boiled.

The Morse-Steinkraus Patent

For several years Professor Keith H. Steinkraus and I collaborated on a mead project. The result was U.S. patent 3,598,607 granted to us on August 10, 1971. For a short while we had hopes of licensing someone to make mead, but the dramatic increase in the world price of honey in 1971 and again in 1973 dashed all hopes of this coming to fruition in the near future. In the 1950's and 1960's the world price of the best grades of honey rose from about eight to nine cents per pound to about fourteen. In mid-1971 the price jumped from fourteen to about thirty cents within a few months, and rose again, to about forty-five cents, in 1973. Recently we have seen another slight increase. Before the 1970's, there was always a small surplus of honey on the world market, while recently we have had a slight shortage. My friends in agricultural economics tell me that a one per cent shortage of a stable food product will cause the price to rise about four per cent.

In our patent we brought together the best of literature on fermentation and our own observations. We aimed at a rapid fermentation and to produce a mead with 12 to 14 per cent alcohol. The following materials are suggested for each gallon of honey-water:

citric acid	18.9 grams
ammonium sulphate	4.65 · "
potassium phosphate	1.9 "
magnesium chloride	0.7 "
peptone	0.1 "
sodium hydrogen sulphate	0.2 "
thiamine	20.0 milligrams
calcium pantothenate	10.0 "
inositol	7.5 "
pyridoxine	1.0 "
biotin	0.05 "

The process[3] calls for careful control of the pH and the fermentation temperature. It is geared to commercial production. A specific yeast selected by us is used. The patent lists three other formulae not too dissimilar to the above.

Metheglin

Many of the recipes for making honey wine call for the addition of herbs and spices. The use of these materials is quite natural as they are widely used in cooking to stimulate the appetite and to improve the flavor of certain bland foods.

Whereas many spiced meads, properly called metheglin, were made to delight the palate, I strongly suspect that spices were also often used to cover faulty fermentations. As is discussed elsewhere, it was not until Pasteur's research in the mid-1800's that the process of wine making was understood and that people learned to use fermentation valves properly and to prevent the growth of harmful bacteria, molds, and yeasts.

I have never compiled a list of herbs and spices that might be used in metheglin making, but a visit to any grocery store will

---

[3]There are obviously many substitutions one may make in this formula. A mixture of citric acid and sodium citrate rather than citric acid alone is better when light honey is used. Four grams of dried yeast extract may be substituted for the last five items.

turn up a seemingly endless number of plant seeds, stems, flowers, leaves, fruits, roots, and combinations thereof for adding flavor to this food or that. I presume a true herbalist is one who grows his or her own products. In most recipes I have read, it appears that blends are especially popular.

Johnston[4] has prepared an excellent article on the subject, and while he does not reveal his own favorite concoctions, he does offer some rules to be followed in making metheglin. The most important of these is that the best flavor results from steeping for up to 24 hours. Longer steepings, leaving the herbs in the fermenting (or fermented) wine, may extract certain bitter components. I presume the length of steeping time will vary from one herb to another. Johnston suggests that one may predict, to a limited degree, the flavor to be obtained by steeping dried herbs in a honey-water-alcohol solution for a given period of time and carefully tasting after about three days. He does encourage the use of two or three items at one time. Some of the "early ideas" might be hyssop and sweet woodruff, rosemary and thyme, and cardomon seed, lemon mint and sweet woodruff. Others that might be used include camomile, rose hips, Asiatic ginger, and sweet basil. I have observed that cinnamon, cloves, and nutmeg are also popular. Still other herbs and spices that might be used are mentioned in the first chapter in some of the early recipes.

When does one add the spices? This is as variable as mead making itself. In Poland I have observed that herbs and spices are added when the honey-water mixture is boiled; they are then removed after the liquid has cooled. Some mead makers add these materials just before the fermentation, but again, long exposure may cause bitter components to be extracted. Alcohol aids the extraction of certain flavors, and it is possible to steep the desired mixture in a finished mead for whatever one considers the proper length of time.

---

[4]Johnston, James W., Jr. The mead maker uses herbs. The Herbarist 39:42-49. 1973.

Fruit meads

Meads using ten to fifty per cent fruit juice have been popular in many countries for many centuries. Probably the most popular juice to mix with honey has been apple, but it is not difficult to find references to the use of pear, plum, peach, raspberry, and other juices.

Most fruit juices will have a low pH suitable for fermentation though measurement of the pH with colored paper strips is appropriate to make certain this is the case. Fruit juice adds nutrients to the medium, usually making it unnecessary to add more nutrients. Adding acid may be helpful, depending upon the amount and type of fruit juice used.

The chief problem with using fruit juice is determining its sugar content and adjusting the quantity of honey. Adding the pulp from the juice makes the use of a hydrometer difficult, if not meaningless.

Apple juice contains ten to twelve per cent sugar. Tart apples make better meads (and ciders) than do the sweet, out-of-hand eating apples. In many countries (notably England), apples are grown specifically for the flavor of the cider they produce. (Outside of the United States cider is usually an alcoholic drink. The grape is an unusual fruit and much higher in sugar than are most fruits, which have from eight to fifteen per cent sugar. If one wishes to make a fruit mead, it is my personal feeling that fifteen to twenty per cent apple juice added to a honey-water mixture is best. The addition of apple juice may aid in stabilizing the final product but will not prevent the slow deposition of protein from the honey. For this reason I suggest the honey-water mixture should be boiled before the fruit juice is added.

Hops in mead making

Hops are never used in making grape wine, but are almost always used in beer manufacture. There are several mead recipes that call for the addition of hops but they are little used in making commercial mead. Hops add a distinctive flavor to any beverage, and whether or not they should be included in mead recipes is a good question.

Hop plants are grown throughout the world. There are male and female hop plants. The pollen is carried by the wind from the male plants to the flowers on the females; it is common to plant one male plant for each 200 female plants. In the northern hemisphere hops flower in July. The female inflorescence, upon fertilization, forms a hop cone or burr. A hop cone may form without fertilization but will ripen more evenly if the flower is fertilized. The ripe hops are harvested in September in the northern hemisphere.

Hops contain resins, oils, tannins, and pectins, all of which help clarify and stabilize alcoholic beverages. It is undoubtedly because of these qualities that hops were first used in making beer, and the fact that hops were good flavoring agents was probably secondary, at least in the beginning.

Clarification and stabilization are not generally a problem with grape wines, but meads are notoriously difficult to clear and inclined to develop haze in time. Hops will aid in clarification and thus they were used in many early mead recipes. We now know that boiling the honey-water mixture before fermentation solves the problem, but hops may add variety to one's meads. It is said that if they are used in small quantity there is little effect on the flavor after some aging; I cannot testify to the truth of this statement. In many ways the use of hops in mead making is akin to the use of herbs and spices, which is discussed above.

Boiling the honey-water mixture

Many of the recipes for making mead, dating from the 1400's through the 1900's, advise that the honey be diluted with water and the resulting mixture be boiled for 30 to 60 minutes. Any scum that rises to the top should be removed, say these recipes. Why is the solution boiled?

If one makes mead without boiling, the fermentation is rapid and the resulting mead will clear, usually after three to four months, but it may never become brilliantly clear. After the new mead is bottled and has aged for six months or more, a precipitate often forms in the bottle and the mead becomes cloudy. The precipitate is formed by proteins originating in the honey. Honeys vary in the quantity of protein they contain, and the meads made from them vary in the quantity of protein they may precipitate in time. Clover honey contains very little protein, and a deposit may not develop in a bottle of mead made from clover honey, without boiling, even after a year or more. Buckwheat, wild thyme, and goldenrod contain much protein-aceous material and will form a heavy deposit. The major reason for boiling the honey-water mixture is to precipitate the proteins in honey and to make a brilliantly clear mead.

One problem with boiling the honey-water mixture is that the flavor is affected by so doing; however, some people prefer the flavor that boiling imparts to the mead. A more important problem is that boiling removes certain of the growth substances needed by the yeast cells to ferment the new mead. If one boils the honey and water, additional yeast food must be added; this is most easily done by adding fruit juice, but doubling the quantity of yeast food to be added will accomplish essentially the same thing.

Boiling the honey and water before fermentation is still popular today. It is practiced in two of the large mead-making establishments I have visited in Poland. It is also done by many home mead makers, especially those who value a clear, brilliant mead. Most people prefer clear meads and wines over cloudy ones, but still, those who prefer the well-aged red wines, burgundy that is 15 to 20 years old, for example, will testify that almost none is without a precipitate.

The diluted honey-water is still an acid medium that will attack any raw metal it contacts, including iron and zinc. Thus, the honey-water should be boiled only in stainless steel or glass vessels.

VI.

Fermenting, Racking and Aging

Making mead, or any alcoholic beverage, is a slow, complex process. Despite much research in many countries, no one has devised any practical method for speeding up the fermentation and/or aging process.

During the fermentation and aging of a mead, many precipitates are formed. Most of these are made up of dead yeast cells. The process of separating the new mead from these cells and the debris that accumulates during the fermentation is called racking. It involves siphoning off the clear liquid from the settlings. It must be done promptly and carefully, as disintegrating dead yeast cells impart off flavors that may ruin an otherwise good mead. Racking may be done several times between fermentation and bottling.

New meads are not palatable. We know that the aging process is a chemical one, and while it is true that chemical processes are speeded up by high temperatures, we are also aware that aging at high temperatures results in a product with a poor flavor. The best meads (and in fact the best wines, as far as I'm aware) develop when they are held at temperatures in the mid 60's. Fluctuating temperatures should be avoided, too.

Home wine makers have found that they may start two or more fermentations with identical formulas, the same yeast, and still end up with wines that taste different. More frequently, two identically treated carboys or barrels may end up with wines with different sugar levels. It is not uncommon for home-made wines to have one or two per cent residual sugar and still have an alcohol content so low that, in theory at least, it should not have prevented further fermentation.

The primary fermentation

When a fermentation is properly conducted it lasts fourteen to twenty-eight days, sometimes as few as ten days. During the fermentation, all, or nearly all, of the sugar is converted into carbon dioxide and alcohol. The alcoholic concentration continues to increase until it is sufficiently high to kill the yeast cells. A residual, or left-over, sugar content of less than one per cent is considered desirable.

When air bubbles are no longer visible passing through the fermentation valve, the mead maker knows the fermentation has ended; the yeast cells die and settle to the bottom of the fermentation container. This marks the completion of the stage known as the primary fermentation, or simply the fermentation. Under ideal conditions there is but one fermentation. Except when making champagne, secondary fermentations should be avoided, but before one discusses these it is necessary to define them.

The term secondary fermentation has a variety of meanings, depending upon the circumstances. In times past, when wine was made in the cellar of an unheated house, or at least a house with a cool cellar, the fermentation often stopped because of cold weather in the fall. The yeast cells settled and the wine became clear despite the fact that there was still much sugar to be fermented. A second fermentation started in the spring when the cellar warmed and the yeast culture began to grow again. It should be remembered that years ago many homes had vegetable cellars that would not freeze but would reach temperatures in the 30's (°F.) during the colder months of the year. Yeast cells will not reproduce at these low temperatures and, in fact, the cultures usually stop growing when the temperature falls into the 40's. This is one circumstance under which the use of the term secondary fermentation arose; this is to be remembered when reading the older literature on wine, or when talking to people who still make wine under such conditions. Further, one should not downgrade making wine in such a fruit or vegetable cellar, for some great wines have been made under primitive conditions. Modern wine technology indicates, however, that temperature control and bringing the fermentation to an end as soon as possible eliminates many dangers, especially from microbes that would adversely affect the wine; thus, controlled conditions are recommended.

The term secondary fermentation may also refer to a fermentation that stopped (stuck) and started again under conditions other than cool winter weather. The reasons for fermentations so stopping are discussed below under Stuck meads.

Lastly, champagne makers also refer to the second fermentation, but this is a desirable fermentation that takes place in the bottle, and is the fermentation that produces the carbon dioxide that gives champagne its bubbles. This is discussed in chapter VIII, under the title Sparkling Mead.

The first racking

The fermentation will stop two to four weeks after it starts; two to four weeks after this, the new wine will begin to clear. Some dead yeast cells will settle to the bottom of the carboy or barrel as the fermentation progresses, but the amount will increase rapidly as the wine clears. At this time the new wine should be racked, or separated from the settlings, which are called lees. It may be necessary to rack the wine three or four times, usually at about three-month intervals. Several precautions must be taken during the racking process.

The sulfur dioxide content of the new wine should be kept high to protect it against infection. A chemical analysis for free sulfur dioxide may be done, but most home wine makers lack the equipment for such an analysis. As a rule of thumb if one adds sulfur dioxide powder or tablets at the outset of the fermentation, it should be at the rate of 50 parts per million. At the time of the first racking, the sulfur dioxide content of the new wine is usually high enough to protect it. However, at the second racking, and again at bottling, the same quantity of chemical as was first used should be added again. This means dosing the wine two or three times before bottling, over a period of about a year. Those who are in a hurry and bottle their wines sooner may use sulfur dioxide only twice.

It is repetitious to say so again, but sulfur dioxide should be no substitute for cleanliness during the racking process.

At the end of the first racking the neck of the newly filled container should have only an inch or so of headspace under the fermentation valve. Exposure to more oxygen than this could lead to spoilage. Also, the fermentation valve should be left in place for two or three months after the first racking. Sometimes a small amount of residual sugar may ferment slowly over a period of a month or more. If the container is tightly bunged, the cork may be forced out or the container may burst.

No matter what the size of the first fermentation container, there will not be enough wine to fill a container of the same size

9. Decanting is being done here with plastic tubing. Care is being taken to prevent adding too much oxygen in the process. Photo by E. S. Phillips.

at the end of the first racking. Thus it is advisable to have a smaller container of wine fermenting at the same time from which to fill the container into which the wine is first racked. An alternative is to have small storage vessels into which the wine is placed. One inventive soul I know filled the container by pouring several handfulls of clean glass marbles into the wine until the volume of wine reached the neck of the carboy.

The easiest method of racking wine from one container to another is to siphon it through a clean plastic hose about five or six feet long. The hose may be soaked in sterilizing (water) solution containing sulfur dioxide for several hours before use; after this, clean water should be allowed to run through it for several minutes.

The mead should not be allowed to splash into the new container for it may incorporate too much oxygen if this is done. The siphon should be held carefully so that the lees are not siphoned over into the racked wine. The home wine maker is usually forced to throw away the lees and a small amount of wine. Commercially the lees are filtered and the wine in them is saved; more frequently they are distilled to make alcohol for fortification. Home filters may be useful but it is probably not a good idea to add the filtered wine to the better wines in the cellar.

The second and subsequent rackings

The purpose of the second and subsequent rackings is to clear the new wine further. The same sanitary precautions urged for the first racking are still important. A major problem with racking is that a small volume is lost each time, necessitating the use of smaller and smaller carboys or barrels.

Methods of fining or clearing wine have been developed. However, as carefully as these might be done, it is still better to avoid the process and to try to obtain a perfectly clear product through several rackings. The final racking should take place at least three months before bottling. During these last three months the wine should remain bright and clear; if it does so, the stability needed for prolonged storage in the bottle has been attained.

Stuck meads

In a normal fermentation, yeast cells feed, grow, and divide. In theory, and because reproduction is by budding and is asexual, the organisms should live forever. However, most yeast cells, like all organisms, do die. Obviously not all do so, for there are always some, somewhere, to carry on another fermentation.

A fermentation that does not go to completion is termed a "stuck" fermentation. A stuck fermentation is one in which, for some reason, the yeast culture dies out before the fermentation is finished.

Stuck fermentations were at one time rather common in the commercial wine-making industry. The fermentation process is exothermic; that is, heat is given off during the fermentation process. This may cause the temperature of the fermenting wine to rise to above 85°F. in a large tank and may kill the yeast cells or slow their growth. It is for this reason that commercial wineries that ferment wines in tanks or vats containing thousands of gallons are continually cooling the must during the fermentation process.

Stuck meads are much less common with the home wine maker, for seldom does the fermenting reach a temperature high enough to kill the growing yeast cells. However, stuck meads do occur and may be due to a faulty or poor yeast culture, too high a sulfur dioxide content, or, rarely, a deficiency in nutrients. A low temperature may halt the fermentation process but usually the fermentation will start again when the temperature rises. An example of a nutritional deficiency is that while yeast cells are capable of synthesizing their own vitamins, they do so at a rather slow rate. It is for this reason that commercial champagne producers have found it advantageous to add vitamins for the second fermentation in the bottle. It is also known that as dead yeast cells disintegrate, after having settled out from the must, vitamins may be liberated back into the fermenting solution and be reused. However, dead yeast cells may also impart off-flavors to the new wine, so wines are racked as soon as they start to clear.

Because a stuck fermentation may occur, the home wine maker should check his wines for sugar content when he racks them. The test takes only a few minutes using a home test kit devised for diabetics and available from drug stores. If a stuck fermentation occurs, the only solution is to reinoculate the must and allow the fermentation to go to completion. Reinoculation is dangerous because of the possibility of contamination and the usual sanitary precautions should be followed; however, the wine maker has no choice and the fermentation should be started as soon as possible.

Aging

Aging is a complex process. During this time the mead clears and certain desirable changes take place in the color, odor, and flavor; it is the changes in the flavor that are especially important. As the mead ages, the dead yeast cells settle and, as indicated elsewhere, it is important that the mead be racked to remove it from the lees (dead yeast cells and other settled material).

Oxygen is important during the aging process, but too much oxygen can cause trouble. The casks or carboys should be kept full as the mead ages. Equally important, one must be careful not to allow too much aeration as the mead is racked. As the mead flows from one container to another in a siphon it should not splash. Light (white) meads (and wines) can be damaged by excessive oxygen much more easily than dark meads (or red wines). In commercial operations it has been found that the misuse of pumps and filling machines (which allow the wine to splash into the bottle) can cause too much oxygen to be added and give off-flavors.

From the point of view of the chemist, aging involves oxidation, reduction, and esterification. All of these processes have been studied extensively, often with the view of speeding up the aging process. No one has yet devised any system that is both fast and satisfactory, so aging a mead or wine today is as time-consuming as it was many years ago.

During the aging process the wine or mead becomes smooth and mellow. Often new mead is harsh and has an unpleasant taste. There is a decrease in acidity during aging. More noticeable than anything else is the development of a pleasant bouquet and fragrance.

Aging in wooden casks has been popular for centuries. The advantage of a cask is said to be that oxygen will enter the wine slowly through the wood; also, as some of the wine evaporates, oxygen will be absorbed from the head space that is created. Many home wine makers use glass exclusively and feel that enough oxygen enters the mead as it is racked. Admittedly, barrels add to the romantic atmosphere of a winery, even if it be one's own cellar.

How long a mead should age is a good question. Light meads and wines age and become palatable much more rapidly than do darker ones. The aging of sweet meads requires more time, too. The higher the alcoholic content of a beverage the longer the aging time needed. I have allowed many light meads to age five and six years, and have felt they have been greatly improved over those aged for a shorter period.

Temperature is important in aging. Yeast cells settle more rapidly at lower temperatures. Fluctuating temperatures should be avoided. It is best to keep the temperature of the area where the aging is done below 70°F. (21°C.). Many authorities agree that 60°F. (15°C.) is a good aging temperature.

Meads that will not clear

Many meads made without boiling the honey-water mixture will not become clear even after standing for a year. Fortunately, this does not occur very often, but when it does it can be a great frustration. Natural clarification and racking three or four times is certainly to be preferred over other methods to bring about clarification. One must make certain that cloudy meads are not clouded because of bacterial contamination and spoilage; spoiled meads cannot be saved. Cloudiness is most commonly caused by proteins that continue to precipitate over a long time.

There are four basic methods of forcing cloudy wines and meads to clear: chilling, heating, fining, and filtering. While filtration is an excellent technique to give mead or wine a brilliantly clear appearance, the equipment necessary for proper filtration is usually practical only for commercial wineries. Small filters must be used with care as they may aerate a wine too much.

Placing a cloudy mead in a refrigerator at a temperature just slightly above freezing for 24 to 48 hours will sometimes force the proteins in solution to precipitate. (This may also hasten the deposition of cream of tartar with certain grape wines.) Certainly, chilling is the easiest of the techniques used for clarification, when it will work, which is not always. Home wine makers may care to experiment with a small quantity of cloudy wine, perhaps a pint or a quart, to determine its reaction to cold temperatures.

Similarly, heating a wine to about the pasteurization temperature, roughly 140° to 145°F. (60° to 62°C.), may also cause proteins to precipitate and will additionally stabilize and pasteurize the wine. However, heating a wine in bulk, that is, in an open container, is not advisable. Commercially, when heating is used as part of the stabilizing process, the wines are heated in a flash pasteurizer; in such a pasteurizer the wine remains within a closed system. In the process, the wine passes between two metal plates heated with hot water and the wine is held at a high temperature for only a brief period of time, usually not more than a minute or two. Home wine makers have been known to make glass coils that they immerse in hot water baths to accomplish the same thing. However, this technique is not easy, and wines may be overheated. There must be a steady flow of wine through the coils to prevent burning.

Many wine makers, both home wine makers and commercial operators, fine their wines. Most will agree that the process does little or no harm, and fining will give the wine a sparkle. The American public prefers a clear wine, and thus commercial wine producers are usually forced to fine their wines. Fining may, however, be avoided, and when this is possible, it is suggested that the home wine maker do so.

The more popular fining agents include bentonite, isinglass, egg white, gelatin, and casein. These materials usually combine, physically or chemically, with the proteins in solution and cause them to precipitate. The clear wine may then be decanted. Certain of the fining agents may also remove color; there is less of a problem with egg albumin and isinglass in this regard than there is with the other fining agents. One problem with all the fining agents is that even after prolonged settling, a large amount of wine is usually discarded in the residue by the home wine maker. Commercial wine makers filter the fining agents from the wine and thus are able to recover almost all of the wine. It is difficult to state how much fining agent should be used to clarify a wine; this depends upon the quantity of material to be removed from the wine. It may be advisable for the home wine maker to experiment with a small quantity of wine to avoid over-fining.

Isinglass is usually considered the best of the fining agents. Usually 0.5 to 1 ounce of isinglass is used per 100 gallons of wine. Small, pre-weighed quantities of isinglass for the home wine maker, together with instructions, are available from some home wine suppliers. The isinglass must first be soaked in cold wine for about 24 hours. Any pieces of isinglass that do not dissolve should be discarded. The isinglass is added to the wine slowly, and it is usually necessary to stir it into the wine carefully, but thoroughly. Settling requires a period of one to two days before the wine is racked.

Egg albumin is a popular fining agent for the home wine maker. Usually, the whites of fresh eggs are used. The white of one egg will fine 10 to 20 gallons of wine. The egg albumin is added to a small amount of water or wine and beaten thoroughly so as to be in suspension before it is added to the wine. Again, it is necessary to mix the fining agent with wine thoroughly. The wine is allowed to settle for a day or two before it is decanted.

Gelatin is available in various grades and only a pure food gelatin should be used to fine a wine. One ounce of gelatin is all that is necessary to fine 100 gallons of wine. The gelatin should first be blended with a very small quantity of wine and then mixed thoroughly with the wine to be fined. As in the case of other fining agents, the sediment forms slowly. It is sometimes helpful to add a small amount of enological tannin to the gelatin to hasten the settling process (especially with white wines). Where tannin is used, it is used in equal quantities with the gelatin.

Casein, like gelatin, is available in several qualities and only the very best casein should be used for fining wines. Three to five ounces of casein are used for 100 gallons of wine. The major drawback with the use of casein is that it will also decolorize wine.

All fining agents are used at cellar temperature. While increasing the temperature may hasten the settling process, it may also have deleterious effects on the new wine.

VII.

Bottling and Closures

If a home mead maker has a supply of bottles that look alike and have good closures, his product will look much more professional. Too often I have been presented a bottle of presumably good mead in a secondhand wine or whiskey bottle of such an odd shape or color that the two were in harmonious to an offensive degree. Worse still is to use the original closure a second time. The advent of the modern shops for home wine-making supplies has eliminated many of the problems once associated with obtaining bottles and other supplies.

Bottles

Tradition dictates that certain wines should be placed in bottles of specific types and colors. The chianti bottle, with its surrounding wicker basket, is well known to wine drinkers. Sauterne wines are stored in long-necked bottles, while Rhine wines are kept in tall, thin bottles. Champagne requires a special bottle because of the pressure under which it is kept. White wines are usually in white or light green glass bottles. Red wines are more frequently kept in dark green (unfortunately, since red wines often make a fine appearance in white glass). The home wine maker is free to follow tradition or not, as he chooses, but there are a few precautions.

New bottles often contain dust. In commercial wineries this is usually blown from the bottles by a jet of air just before they are filled. In commercial practice wine bottles are not washed, although it might be good if they were. The home wine maker should wash his bottles with a good alkaline soap, and rinse them carefully so that no soap film will adhere to the glass.

Just before the mead is placed in the bottles, they should be rinsed with a newly made sulfur dioxide and water solution. A solution with about 200 parts per million of sulfur dioxide will help to insure a clean bottle. Where bottles are being reused, and most home wine makers reuse their bottles many times, they should be cleaned carefully. Some people advise sterilizing in a dry oven or boiling in water, but I don't think this is really necessary.

In selecting a stardard bottle for one's own cellar, it is necessary to think about the type of closure to be used. This is especially true where long corks are preferred. Some bottles, especially the long-necked bottles often used for Rhine wines, may have a neck that spreads too much. The neck interior should be of uniform inside diameter for the length that will be filled with cork.

Probably the best "all-around" bottle for the home mead maker is the white glass, long-necked bottle commonly associated with Sauterne-type wines. Almost any wine looks good in this type of bottle. It is a broad base and will not tip over easily. Most such bottles take a cork with ease and hold it well; many will also take a screw cap. In such a bottle one can easily check for deposits, off-colors, and spoilage.

Plastic bottles are being used for packaging some foods. So far as I am aware, none has been shown to be satisfactory for wine. Plastic corks are also available, especially for champagne bottles. Research in Germany indicates these leak too much oxygen. Off flavors are also a problem, or at least are thought to be.

A last piece of advice concerning bottling is about over-aeration and too long exposure of the new mead to the air when it is bottled. Advice on this subject is too often of the "do as I say, not as I do" nature! The best thing to suggest is that everything be made ready in advance and that the bottling proceed as rapidly as .possible with as little exposure to air as one can manage.

Headspace

Headspace is that space in a bottle between the cap or cork and the contents. It is little mentioned in the literature but can be of prime consequence insofar as keeping qualities of a mead or wine are concerned. Commercial wineries are directed by federal regulations to fill their bottles uniformly and to fill them to the volume indicated on the label. The home wine maker is at liberty to be more precise, and to fill the bottles to enhance the keeping qualities of the mead.

There should be as little headspace in a bottle as possible. Several times more oxygen may be absorbed from the air in a large headspace than is absorbed during the final racking and bottling process. If the distance between the mead and the cork is approximately one-half to three-quarters of an inch, the bottle is properly filled. Corking bottles fuller than this is difficult and, in fact, should not be done. Commercially, where crown caps, screw caps, and foils are used, the headspace may often be 2 to 2½ inches long. This usually does little harm to red wines, but white wines may absorb too much oxygen. Still, a bottle of mead closed with a crown or screw cap and with only half an inch of headspace does not give a good appearance. This appears to be another good reason for using a cork. A corked bottle with a small headspace makes a fine appearance.

Screw caps

Screw caps are popular for wine bottles, both commercially and home bottled. I don't happen to like them. Part of this prejudice concerns storage, and the fact that screw caps do not give good protection for more than a year. Often screw caps will show signs of rust after several months in a cellar; this may be prevented by placing a bit of vaseline on the cap (on the outside, not on the inside) or by dipping the capped end of a bottle in beeswax or paraffin.

Where wines are stored for only a short time, a plastic lining in the screw cap will probably do no harm. However, caps with plastic linings should be tested before they are used extensively, and such testing requires long-term exposure. Screw caps lined with cork, if they can be obtained, are better. Caps, like bottles, may be dusty, and should be washed before they are used. Rinsing caps in a sulfur dioxide solution is an easy method of sterilization.

Crown caps

Crown caps, of the type used on ordinary soft-drink bottles, are little used by home wine makers but are to be preferred over screw caps. The reasons for this are twofold and simple: First crown caps seat better and more firmly, and second, the cork in crown caps, even though it contains glue, does not give the wine an off flavor. It is slightly helpful, but not necessary, to place the capped bottles on their sides to keep the cork moist. However, this is not too important and should not be confused with or

10. *A capper for crown caps. Crown caps are satisfactory when making sparkling mead.*

11. A rusty crown cap. Caps of this nature are effective closures. A small amount of vaseline prevents rusting.

even considered in the same light as the proper use of real wine corks.

Crown caps are available from many sources and cappers cost only a few dollars. Like screw caps, crown caps may show signs of rust in a damp cellar but they may be protected by a coating of vaseline or paraffin. Special bottles are required for crown caps and this discourages their use by many home wine makers. Many champagne bottles will take crown caps. Most champagne makers who conduct the second fermentation in the bottle use only crown caps during this fermentation. Crown caps will hold several atmospheres of pressure with ease and, from a practical point of view, are perfectly satisfactory.

Corks and corking

In my opinion a cork, a good clean cork about two inches long, should be used to close a bottle of mead. It looks better, it is better; it makes it possible for the wine to have a long life in the

*12-13. A corking machine for seating a two-inch-long cork.
Corks are the traditional closures for wine and mead bottles.*

bottle. Corks aid in aging. In fact, I can't remember anyone's ever giving any good reason why a cork should not be used! Corks may deteriorate with great age, but there are ways to slow this process and to give the corks some protection. However, corks may be misused and some advice on how to cork a bottle properly is necessary. I, like everyone else who has ever used corks, have made mistakes, but these are easy to avoid once the corking process is understood.

Corks are cut from the thick bark of the cork oak. Cork oaks may live to be 200 or more years old; the bark is removed every nine or ten years, and if the cambium layer of the tree is not broken, the tree will live and new bark will form. Good wine corks will show at least seven growing rings, or will be made by laminating (gluing) two or more pieces together, as is commonly done with champagne corks. The demand for cork is great and appears to exceed the supply slightly, thus the high price and the fact that many commercial firms are forced to seek substitutes.

The wine maker should be prepared to throw away a small percentage of the corks from each batch purchased. It is just not worthwhile to try to save a few pennies by using a cork that does not appear perfect. Corks with hard lumps or bumps that can be seen or felt on the surface are to be avoided. Corks will sometimes have dark streaks of outer bark visible; these may contaminate the wine. Corks with long streaks, indentations, or grooves along one side should be discarded, as these may make a pathway through which too much oxygen or contamination may enter. Even under the best circumstances bits and pieces of the cork may fall into the wine; these do little harm.

New corks may be dusty, and bacteria and yeasts have been cultured from the cracks and crevices in corks. Thus, most people attempt to sterilize the corks as much as possible before they are used; in practical terms this is difficult if not impossible.

14. The bottle on the left was not designed for a cork. The neck tapers on the inside and as a result mead has leaked along the side of the cork. The bottle on the right does not taper on the inside and holds the cork firmly.

Cheap corking machines or gadgets are not satisfactory to force a cork into a bottle. If one can put a cork, say a tapered cork, into a bottle by hand, the cork is too small. Only a cork made for wine bottles is satisfactory, and such corks must be compressed and forced into the neck of the bottle. A good corking machine will grasp and hold the neck of the bottle when it is being corked. In the corking process the corks are first compressed and then forced into the neck of the bottle with a plunger. This is a problem, for not all corking machines are strong enough to compress a dry cork. Soaking corks, so they may be compressed with ease, usually means that some of the soaking solution contaminates the wine. Many wine hand-books advise soaking the cork in a strong sulfur dioxide solution (200 or more parts per million) for about one hour prior to use. Glycerin is usually added; this helps the corks slip into place. They next advise wiping the underside of the cork dry with an absorbent cloth after the cork is compressed in the

15. This cork is properly seated about one-sixteenth of an inch below the top of the bottle.

corking machine and just before it is forced into the bottle. Commercial firms blow a jet of air over the cork tip after compression and before the plunger drives the cork into place.

How then does one proceed? It is first advisable to keep the corks in a clean, dry storage area. Bacteria and harmful microbes are less common and will not grow in a dry area. Corks may be soaked in a sulfur dioxide solution and then dried or partially dried several days before they are used. A light coating of paraffin or beeswax will give the cork some protection and help it slide into place. Such a light wax coating will slow, but will not prevent, the wine resting against the cork from entering the cork and forcing it to swell. The cork must swell and expand against the glass to give the wine the protection it needs.

Paraffin or beeswax is put onto the cork by tumbling. To tumble, corks and one or more pieces of wax are placed in a clean container that is revolved on a spit, usually for about an hour. The tumbling action should be slow and gentle. If the cork is tumbled too rapidly, large deposits and lumps of wax will form on the cork, and this is not desirable. The precise time the tumbling should take depends on how much wax is in the tumbler. Not only is wax deposited from the large piece of wax onto each cork, but as corks come in contact with each other the wax is redistributed, thus making a fine, even coat of wax over all the corks.

Newly corked bottles of wine must be left in an upright position for two to three days after corking. This must be done because the air in the bottle is compressed during the corking and this compressed air should be allowed to leak out. If this air does not leak out, the pressure in the bottle may force a small amount of wine out of the bottle between the glass and the cork. This happens especially with heavily waxed corks before the corks have time to swell and prevent this loss. The greatest danger is that the pathway so created may be a route for bacteria to enter the bottle. More commonly, the leaked wine evaporates

16. Another type of machine for corking. The cork must be compressed to fit into the bottle. Photo by Paul Comer.

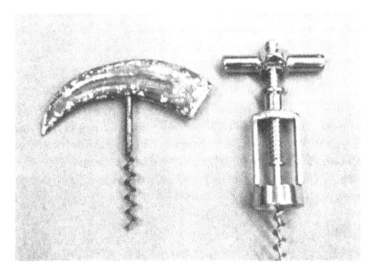

17. Corkscrews. The type on the right exerts a slow, positive pressure on the cork and is preferred.

on the exposed end of the cork and is attacked by mold and bacteria. This seldom causes trouble except when the wine is stored for a long period of time. However, mold growing on the cork is unsightly.

The cork should be seated one-eighth to one-sixteenth of an inch below the top of the bottle.

Very rarely, insects (in the larval stage, usually) will attack a cork. This occurs so infrequently as to be scarcely worth mentioning, but long papers have been written on the subject. Insecticides are little used in a winery. A clean, tight cellar is the best protection against insect damage. Dipping the tip of the bottle in beeswax has been advised as protection against insect attack. It may also serve to give the final package a better appearance. Colored waxes are often used.

Two to three days after corking, the wine bottles are placed on their sides and are never again put in an upright position until they are chilled for serving.

Capsules and foils

A metal or plastic foil over the end of the corked bottle improves its appearance and protects the cork against insect attack and discoloration by molds and fungi. Metal foils in various colors are available, as are crimpers to give the foil a uniform appearance after it is pressed into place. Plastic foils, which are packed and sold wet and shrink as they dry, are also available. The plastic seals usually cover about two inches of the end of the bottle and have a life of several years. The use of some encapsulating device is advised, as they have both esthetic and practical value.

Labels

Eye appeal has much to do with what we buy, eat, and drink. Presenting an appealing package is not a subject of concern for the commercial packer only; it can have much to do with what one's friends and neighbors think when tasting a homemade mead.

For reasons already mentioned, it is most logical to present mead in a white or transparent bottle. Most mead is pale yellow to amber in color, reflecting, of course, the color of the honey from which it is made. Both orange and yellow are highly visible in the color spectrum. The colors on the label should complement the color of the bottle's contents. The appearance of the lighter colored meads is enhanced by a label with a red and blue background. A darker mead would have greater eye appeal if the label contained more blue.

A label should contain certain basic information. The word mead should be in large letters, visible from a distance of about ten feet. The label should not be cluttered, but should also give the producer's name and address, and the date it was made. Dr. Steinkraus and I prepared a second label for our mead that tells more about the product and, we hope, arouses greater interest in it.

Mead is not a new drink. Long before the grape was introduced into Northern Europe, honey was the chief sweet and the main source of sugar to make an alcoholic beverage. The Norseman made wine from honey; no doubt the ale and wine that Robin Hood allegedly took from Prince John had honey as its base. In early England and until about 1600, mead was the national drink.

The honey wine in this bottle was made by the natural fermentation of honey diluted with clear water. Nutrients were added to enhance the fermentation, and the yeast was selected from wine yeasts. The wine was aged in oak casks. The type of honey from which this wine was made is shown on the opposite label. The alcohol content is 10 to 12%. This experimental sample is offered for organoleptic testing.

18. A second (back) label, designed to tell the consumer about the product. Such labels give the discriminating taster background that will be of interest.

VIII.

Sparkling Mead

Sparkling wines and meads are prestige items. This has been recognized by state and federal governments that tax them at unusually high rates despite their low alcoholic content. Sparkling beverages can have a superior flavor. Carbon dioxide is used to enhance the taste of many beverages, including soft drinks and beer, as well as champagne. While the reasons for this effect of carbon dioxide are not clear, most people agree that the effervescent nature of the beverage has a great effect on one's taste buds and improves the flavor. The greater the amount of carbon dioxide, the better the flavor.

Most soft drinks and beer contain only a small amount of carbon dioxide under only a few pounds pressure. Champagne, and the most sparkling wines, have three to four atmospheres (45 to 60 pounds) of carbon dioxide. Obtaining this much carbon dioxide in the natural fermentation process is not difficult; however, it is important that the sparkling mead be made and kept only in good bottles that will not explode under such high pressure.

Technically, champagne is a sparkling wine made only in the Champagne District of France. French law states that only certain grapes may be used in its manufacture. To Americans, champagne has a much broader meaning and many wineries call their sparkling wines by this name. However, as the wine industry expands in the United States, other sparkling wines are becoming known and being more widely made.

Sparkling wines can be made by the home wine maker. A thorough knowledge of the wine-making process is required. It is helpful to have equipment available to test the alcoholic content of the wine as well as the sugar content at certain times during the champagne-making process. Most important is obtaining bottles that will stand the high pressure. It is not necessary to use a champagne cork in a bottle of champagne or sparkling wine. An ordinary crown cap will serve just as well. Most champagne bottles will accommodate such a cap. Unfortunately, a crown cap removes some of the romance associated with opening a bottle of champagne.

History

The process for making champagne was discovered, probably by accident, in a monastery in France in the 1700's. It was observed that as winters grew cooler, the fermentations slowed and often stopped. As the weather warmed in the spring, the yeasts would become active again and the wine in the casks might undergo a second fermentation. Wines in containers whose bungholes had been closed might accumulate carbon dioxide from a second fermentation, and thuse give the wine a slight sparkle. Usually, however, the accumulated carbon dioxide blew the bung from the bunghole. The discovery was that one might bottle new wine in midwinter, at a time when the fermentation had stopped, and then in the spring, as the temperature warmed, carbon dioxide would accumulate in the bottle from a second fermentation, and high pressures would develop.

Champagne quickly gained widespread acceptance. It was recognized as a different beverage with rare and exhilerating qualities. From the very beginning, champagne was difficult to make and a rare item on the market, thus its high price. At that time, the process of making glass bottles was crude, and most of the bottles of champagne blew up and were lost. Probably not more than five to ten per cent survived, and even that estimate may be high for the first years. It was soon found that the weakest point of the glass bottle was the bottom, which would blow out with great ease under pressure. Research showed that a bottle with a concave bottom was less likely to blow up.

Our modern understanding of champagne making dates from the middle of the nineteenth century, when the subject was researched by Pasteur. He learned that there must first be a fermentation that forms about ten per cent of the alcohol. After this, the wine must be cleared and there must be a second fermentation in the bottle, which produces an additional two per cent alcohol and the carbon dioxide that gives the champagne its bubbles. However, the sugar content must be controlled for the second fermentation or too much carbon dioxide will be made. Until Pasteur's work, champagne making had been a haphazard process. Some champagnes had so much carbon dioxide that no bottle would hold the pressure. Pasteur learned that precisely the right amount of sugar would produce sufficient carbon dioxide to give the champagne three to four atmospheres of pressure. With this knowledge it was possible for the glass industry to develop a bottle that would usually withstand this much pressure. Still, bottles of champagne blew up, causing great difficulty and sometimes physical harm. It was not until quite recently that the glass industry has been able to design a really safe bottle for champagne. Even today, wrapping a bottle of champagne in a wet, cool towel is a standard practice in some restaurants. Originally, the towel was to protect the consumer and the waiter should his warm hands expand the gas within the bottle just enough to force the bottle to explode. Many people think the towel's only purpose is to keep the bottle cool; perhaps it is just as well that they think this is the case.

The base for a sparkling mead

A sparkling mead is no different from any other mead as regards the quality of the honey with which one starts. As I have indicated elsewhere, we prefer to use the darker, stronger honeys as a base for mead; this is true of sparkling meads as well. The dilution of the honey also dilutes the ingredients that give it its strong flavor. However, I have had sparkling meads made from honey of all colors and flavors. Any fruits that blend well with honey to make an ordinary mead will also lend themselves to the making of a sparkling mead. As in the making of any mead, one should not use capping-melter or bitter honey. The final product will be only as good as the ingredients that go into its manufacture.

How to make sparkling mead

Making a sparkling mead requires two fermentations. The first is conducted in the normal way in a cask or carboy, and the resulting mead is allowed to clear and age for a few months.

After it is clear the new mead is placed in champagne-type bottles. Sugar,[1] nutrients, and yeast are added, and there is a second fermentation in the bottle, which produces additional alcohol and the carbon dioxide that gives the product its bubbles. However, all of these steps must be well understood and precisely done; the order in which these are done is outlined below.

The mead to be made sparkling should contain about 10 per cent alcohol. If there is less than this, the final product will be more difficult to stabilize. If there is much more alcohol than this, the yeast cells, which are introduced to bring about the second fermentation, may not grow. The final alcoholic content is controlled by the initial dilution of the honey. When one is making the base for a sparkling mead, the must should contain about 18 to 19 per cent sugar. Just as important is that all the sugar be fermented. If there is residual sugar in the base to be fermented, and more sugar is added for the second fermentation, there will be too much sugar in the mixture, creating to much pressure and causing the bottle to explode.

In the first step, the mead is fermented normally, allowed to settle, and racked. It is usually not placed in the champagne-type bottles for the second fermentation until it is six months to one year old. After this time it should be taste tested to make certain it is sound. When tasting a young mead it should be remembered that it will not have all the characteristics of a well-aged product, but one can detect off flavors in the early stages. It is advisable to add sulfur dioxide to the new mead before it is placed in bottles for the second fermentation, but care must be taken not to add too much or the fermentation will be affected. One should use only half as much as usual (about 25 parts per million) and, more important, this should be done 12 to 24 hours before the yeast is added, so it does not inhibit yeast growth.

---

[1]In making a sparkling mead I prefer to use sugar for the second fermentation for two reasons: it is easier to control the dose, and no protein, which might precipitate and cause cloudiness, will be present.

19. A home winemaker's cellar. Corked bottles rest on their sides Wooden cases protect the carboys against breakage. Photo by E. S. Phillips.

A few days before the new wine is to be bottled, the yeast culture should be prepared. Only a few drops of an active yeast culture are needed to bring about the second fermentation in the bottle. Special champagne yeasts are desirable, if available. Champagne yeasts are selected for two qualities in addition to the usual characteristics of a good yeast: first is their ability to ferment sugar starting at a higher alcoholic concentration, and second, and perhaps more important, is the settling or agglutinating nature of the dead yeast cells. When the second fermentation in the bottle is finished, the dead yeast cells and any other debris must settle so that they may be removed. Dead yeast cells that settle quickly and form a mass that is easily removed are highly desirable. (Removing the yeast from a bottle of champagne is discussed below.)

Champagne producers make a sugar syrup to be added to the new wine for the second fermentation in exact quantity. An easier method for the home wine maker is to measure the new mead accurately and add the precise amount of sugar to it. This may be done by dissolving the sugar in a small quantity of the new mead, or in water, and stirring this into the new mead with care. Too much stirring may allow too much oxygen to be added, but the sugar must be thoroughly mixed so that there will be equal quantities in all bottles.

The correct amount of sugar to add to one gallon of must to make sparkling mead is 60 grams or two ounces. This would yield a sparkling mead with about four atmospheres of pressure. Each additional half ounce of sugar per gallon of must would yield an additional atmosphere of pressure. A bottle of sparkling mead with much more than four atmospheres of pressure would probably be unsafe to handle.

Some commercial champagne makers add yeast food (nutrients and vitamins) to the bottle to hasten the second fermentation. Slow fermentations are to be avoided since they may not go to completion, and higher alcoholic content gives better disease resistance. Adding nutrients in small quantity to champagne is probably desirable but is not required; if one has a supply of nutrients, they should be used. Many wine supply shops will have nutrients for this precise purpose.

During the bottle fermentation an ordinary crown cap is sufficient to cap the bottle. This, of course, requires a bottle that will take a crown cap. For the second fermentation in the bottle, the bottles are usually placed on their sides. The progress of the fermentation is determined by checking for a deposit of dead yeast cells, a few of which should be visible after a few weeks or a month. The second fermentation should be conducted at normal cellar temperatures. It may take a few weeks to several months to go to completion, and the bottles should not be disturbed for several months, preferably a year. Making a good wine or champagne should not be a hurried process. In the beginning, the home wine maker must conent himself with the thought that taking additional time will produce a better product. After he becomes more knowledgeable, he will be able to predict his mead needs, and make his mead in sufficient quantities to keep a stock on hand. After a year or so, the new sparkling mead may be disgorged.

It is advisable to wear a mask or goggles and heavy gloves while examining a bottle of champagne or sparkling mead. The warmth of the hands may be sufficient to cause a weak bottle to explode. Although the champagne bottles made today are strong and of good quality, even the best of bottles may have weaknesses in the glass that could result in explosions.

Disgorging and sweetening

At the end of the fermentation there is a residue of white, dead yeast cells on the side of the bottle. Removing this sediment is called disgorging. Should one bother to disgorge a bottle made for home consumption? This is a very good question, one that only the mead maker himself can answer. Disgorging can be done at home but it is not easy and no doubt mistakes will be made with the first few bottles.

Disgorging a bottle of sparkling mead is really not necessary. One may take the bottle that has lain on its side during the second fermentation, shake it thoroughly, place it in an upright position, and let the dead yeast cells and deposits within the bottle settle to the bottom. About a week should be sufficient for a thorough settling. When the mead is clear, the bottle may be very carefully placed in the refrigerator and cooled to the proper temperature. Then, when it is time to serve, the bottle should be opened slowly and the contents very carefully poured so the sediment is not disturbed. The fact that the bottle should be opened slowly cannot be overemphasized. The crown cap should be lifted carefully at one point only so that a low "hiss" is heard; otherwise much liquid will be lost and the sediment will be disturbed. After the process of pouring has started, with the sediment still in the bottle, the bottle must not be tipped back into an upright position, but moved from one glass to another until the bottle is nearly empty. A small amount of mead is left in the bottle and discarded. Sediment does not add to the eye appeal in a glass, and may have a bitter taste.

Sparkling mead that is not disgorged will be very dry, presuming, of course, that the fermentation goes to completion. Some people prefer a very dry mead, but most prefer it with one-half to two per cent sugar. If a slightly sweeter drink is desired, it is necessary to disgorge, add sugar syrup and alcohol, recork the bottle, and allow some further aging to take place.

The most difficult part of the disgorging process is getting the dead yeast cells and deposits, which result from the second fermentation, into the neck and against the bottle cap so they may be removed. If the champagne bottles have lain on their sides for a year or more, the deposit within the bottle may cling to the side of the bottle and be difficult to remove. The only method of dislodging the sediment is to shake the bottle thoroughly. A mechanical shaker may be required and is used in commercial operations. Once the sediment is loosened and in suspension, the process known as "riddling" is started. Commercial champagne makers have special riddling racks that can be copied by the home wine maker. Riddling racks should be made so that the bottles can be placed, at first, with the neck down and almost horizontal, and then gradually moved into an upright position. Once the riddling is started it should be continued two or three times a day. The process is to pick up the bottle, give it a quarter of a turn, and drop it back into place with a gentle jar. The riddling should continue for two to three weeks. At the end of this time the bottle should have been worked upright slowly so that at the end of the riddling the bottle is in a position of 90° to the floor, that is, precisely upside down. If the riddling has been carefully done, the yeast cells will all lie in the neck of the bottle and against the bottle cap. One should examine the bottles with a bright light to make sure the mead is clear.

It is best to disgorge a sparkling mead on a cool day or in a cellar where the temperature is not above 45°F. (7°C.) 38 to 40°F. (3° to 5°C.) is probably ideal.

When the bottles are chilled, the necks are placed in a brine of salt and chipped ice so that the sediment and a small amount of mead will freeze in the neck. The neck of the bottle should be inserted into the brine about 1 to 1¼ inches. After the neck of the bottle has been in the brine for about 1 hour, the sediment in the neck should be frozen.

The next step is the most difficult. The bottle should be removed slowly and carefully from the cold brine, tipped at an angle of about 45°, and the cap removed with a bottle opener. If all goes well, the pressure within the bottle will blow the ice plug out of the bottle, taking all the dead yeast cells and sediment with it. One should then place his thumb over the top of the bottle to prevent the escape of any more carbon dioxide.

At this point the so-called "dosage" is added. In commercial wine making the dosage is brandy and sugar. The purpose of the sugar is to sweeten the champagne slightly; the purpose of the brandy is to raise the alcoholic content of the champagne another two to four per cent, sufficiently high to prevent a third fermentation in the bottle, which could cause an explosion. The home wine maker can use a commercial brandy, one as tasteless as possible to avoid affecting the taste of the champagne itself. Some people use a small amount of vodka, sometimes diluted with water, since vodka is about as tasteless as any alcoholic beverage on the market.

It is difficult to advise how much sugar should be added to the final product. The dosage should probably vary between 5 and

15 grams per fifth (a fifth is a bottle that holds 4/5 of a quart). There are 28.6 grams in one ounce.

Usually a certain amount of champagne is lost in the process of disgorging, and it is necessary to have one bottle to use to fill the others. This bottle should be kept chilled so that carbon dioxide will not escape from it while it is open, and it may be corked in between times when a small amount is poured into other bottles to fill them. It is probably advisable to give the new sparkling mead a dosage of sulfur dioxide along with the sugar-brandy mixture.

The final step in the disgorging process is the recapping of the bottles. This may be done with an ordinary crown cap, or a champagne-type cork may be used. Again, the home sparkling mead maker is at a disadvantage because a regular champagne cork requires a stronger-than-average corking machine to force the cork into the bottle. However, an ordinary cork used to cork a bottle of wine is satisfactory. It should be inserted its full lenth into the neck of the champagne bottle and then a metal cap tied over the top so the pressure within the bottle will not force it out. From this point onward the bottle should lie on its side so that the cork remains wet and swollen; if this is not done the cork will dry and the content will be lost.

Following the adding of the dosage and the corking, the new mead needs additional aging so the brandy and sugar may blend with the new wine. This takes at least 6 months; a year is more desirable.

It is generally agreed that the acidity of the mead to make a sparkling product should be high, usually 0.6 to 0.8 percent with most mead makers recommending at least 0.7 per cent acid; those lower in acid have a flat taste. As indicated elsewhere it is best to add a blend of acids; tartaric, citric, and malic are preferred.

Traditionally, champagne is very light in color and has a brilliant appearance; however, I don't think this is too important. Some champagne makers add charcoal to their wine before the fermentation in the bottle. Charcoal will pick up any color, and unfortunately a certain amount of flavor, and may improve the physical appearance of champagne. Charcoal is oftentimes used when red or black grapes are used as a base for champagne and the resulting juice, even after a light pressing, has a slightly reddish tinge. The correct quantity is in the range of three grams of charcoal to five gallons of wine. However, more than any other amelioration practice, the addition of charcoal is probably the most questionable. The chief disadvantage of using charcoal is that a certain amount of flavor may be removed.

Drinking sparkling meads

A special note on drinking sparkling wines is important. Most people serve champagne in wide-mouthed, more or less

20. The glass on the left was designed for a sparkling beverage and causes the rapid release of carbon dioxide as the stem, and the beverage in it, warms. The author prefers to drink champagne from the glass on the right, which allows the slow release of carbon dioxide.

flat glasses. Such glasses warm the liquid and the carbon dioxide is lost rapidly. It is correct that these wide, flat glasses give the champagne a better appearance, but they also ruin its flavor rapidly, making the sparkling wine flat and insipid. If one wanted to drink a wine without carbon dioxide, he should have bought a non-gaseous wine to begin with. Worse still are the hollow-stemmed champagne classes that warm the wine in the stem and cause a constant flow of bubbles to the top. While these may look pretty, they shorten the taste life. In my opinion, champagne should be drunk from ordinary, tulip-shaped wine glasses that will warm it as slowly as possible.

IX.

Diseases and Disorders

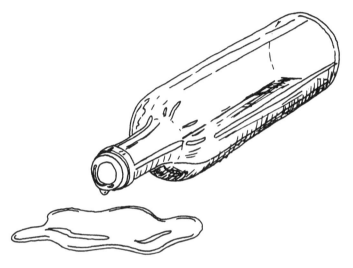

Mead may become hazy or cloudy upon storage. Such changes may result from the natural deposition of protein or some other materials in the wine, or it may be indicative of a disorder or disease. Old wines, especially old red wines, almost invariably have a deposit in the bottles; this does no harm, although the wine should be decanted before it is served. Many species of microorganisms will attack a mead or wine, some feeding on the alcohol, some on the residual sugar, some on the protein, and some on other parts. Contamination with certain metals can also spell trouble. We have a good understanding of wine diseases and disorders today, and spoilage problems are much less common than they were a few decades ago.

The microorganisms that attack wine have two things in common: They are able to tolerate the acidity of the wine, and they are able to tolerate the wine's alcohol. Both acid and alcohol protect the wine against many of the more common bacteria that attack other foods. It is because of this protection by acid and alcohol that wine making is said to be one way of preserving fruit juice. Indeed, before man understood fermentation and the effect of acid and alcohol, most people recognized that a good wine or mead in a sealed barrel or bottle would keep without difficulty.

A few of the more important and common wine disorders are discussed below; several textbooks are devoted to this subject. Identification of the microbes responsible for a bad wine is difficult, even in a commercial laboratory. The home wine maker should recognize that problems may exist. Suffice it to say that sanitation, that is, the use of clean containers, clean siphon tubes, proper fermentation valves, etc., is necessary. Again, taste is one of the best detectors of errors and bad meads. The best defense against harmful microorganisms is the proper use of sulfur dioxide. Careful storage is also very important, including the proper type of bottle, good corks, and storage at low temperatures. Corked bottles should be stored on their side so the mead rests against the cork (see Corks). No harm is done if the wine is off the cork briefly, but the character of a wine in a bottle that sits on a store shelf for weeks or months before it is sold may change appreciably.

Vinegar bacteria

The most serious wine disorder for the home wine maker is caused by the several species of microorganisms known as *Acetobacter*. These bacteria attack the alcohol in wine and turn it into acetic acid, or vinegar. Once done, there is no recovery: the wine must either be used as vinegar or discarded.

Every home wine maker should understand certain fundamentals about the growth of *Acetobacter*. First, it is an aerobic microorganism, that is, it requires oxygen for growth. Thus, barrels or carboys only partially filled are much more subject to attack than those that are filled. Barrels are usually only partly full during the primary fermentation unless an antifoam is used. When the fermentation is completed the barrel must be filled or the contents transferred to another container so the new mead will be properly protected.

The old-fashioned way to make cider vinegar was to fill the barrel about ¾ full of cider and to leave the bung open. A fermentation would start naturally because the juice was contaminated with yeasts. The open bung would allow the entrance of the mother-of-vinegar (*Acetobacter*). The open bung also provided the oxygen necessary for the growth of *Acetobacter*. The microorganism grows best at slightly higher temperatures than are normally used for wine making, usually above 85°F. Years ago, when vinegar was an important home product for preservation, barrels of cider kept in cellars often did not develop into vinegar until the early spring, when the temperature warmed. In the interim, before the taste of the vinegar was too repulsive, the alcoholic content of about seven per cent made the cider palatable.

Fortunately, small quantities of sulfur dioxide will prevent the growth of *Acetobacter* but will not affect the growing yeasts adversely. High-alcohol wines are less subject to attack by *Acetobacter* than are low-alcohol wines, so it is especially important that the proper amount of sulfur dioxide be present at the start of the fermentation.

Ropiness in mead

Some sediments in mead will have a ropy or stringy appearance when the bottle is shaken or disturbed. Such a ropy character is an almost certain sign of bacterial contamination; usually the mead must be discarded. Ropiness is usually caused by one of several lactic acid bacteria, which attack sugar, and sometimes malic acid, and convert it into lactic acid. The resulting wine will have a "mousy" or lactic acid taste, a term given such bad wine by Pasteur over a century ago.

Metallic cloudiness and sediments

Certain metals, notably iron, copper, and, to a lesser extent, aluminum and tin, may cause the formation of sediments or cloudiness in wine; however, this is rare. Papers on the subject indicate the metals may come from spray materials on unwashed grapes; when one examines modern growing practices closely, this seems improbable. More likely, metals coming in contact with the wine during the crushing and pressing processes are to blame for the problem. Commercial practices have been devised to control this type of wine disorder; none of these techniques is especially adapted for the home wine maker.

The best advice for home wine makers is to avoid the use of metal as much as possible. The wine maker will probably have little difficulty with musts that are in contact with metal for only a short period of time. Prolonged contact of the acid must with metal is required for the metal to go into solution. Stainless steel should be used where metal is required.

Protein precipitate

One of the greatest problems in making mead is that a small amount of protein may precipitate, thus clouding it. This precipitate is clearly of fine grain and quite different from the ropy precipitate described above. It has no effect on the flavor, but it does make the mead less appealing to the eye. Its source is the honey used; there is more protein in dark honey than in light honey.

Chilling will sometimes cause the protein in mead to precipitate but it cannot be depended upon. When it is done, the new mead, which may be perfectly clear, is placed in a refrigerator just prior to bottling at about 40°F. for 24 to 48 hours, during which time the precipitate may form.

As indicated earlier, the European method to eliminate this precipitate is to boil the honey-water mixture for about 30 minutes before fermentation. Boiling is mentioned in nearly all of the old literature, and is clearly a long-time tradition. The addition of hops will also prevent protein precipitation, but it will also have a pronounced effect on the flavor and is not a method I advise. The addition of tannin may likewise stabilize the mead; care must be taken when adding tannin that the honey is not naturally high in iron, as this may cause it to darken. Tannin may also impart an off-flavor. Special enological-type tannins are available for those who wish to experiment with them.

X.

Home Analysis and Judging

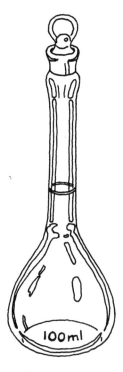

Tasting is really the most important test for the mead maker. In the final analysis a mead is either good or bad by this test. Bad meads cannot be changed. The home mead maker must understand the only thing to do with a bad mead is to throw it away or to make it into vinegar.

Still, in the process of mead making there are several tests that can serve as guides to help the mead maker determine where he may be wrong (or right!). Some of the tests described below are simple and require little apparatus, while others are complicated and require equipment not easily obtained. Specializing in wine analyses for one's self and friends is an avocation within an avocation. Once the basic techniques are understood, the analyses are routine and require only time and continued care.

Residual sugar

The urine-sugar analysis sets available in most drug stores are a boon for the home wine maker. While they were not designed to test for sugar in mead or wine, they are excellent for this purpose. The kits usually come with a test tube, eye-dropper, a bottle of tablets, and a color chart. A few drops of mead are added to some water in the test tube and a tablet is dropped into the solution. A reaction takes place within about 15 seconds, and one may then compare the color in the test tube with the color chart to determine how much sugar is present. The charts allow the home wine maker to determine lower levels of sugar more accurately than higher levels; the charts usually read in gradients of zero, one-quarter, one-half, three-quarters, one, and two per cent sugar.

The level of sugar a home mead maker wants varies. Often one's wife will prefer a slightly sweeter mead. A series of tests will indicate what is preferred both in purchased and home-made products. It is also interesting to experiment to determine what level of sugar in mead one is able to detect with his tongue. Levels of one and two per cent are easily detected by most people; it is more difficult to tell the difference between a mead with no sugar and one-quarter or one-half per cent sugar.

Wines and meads should first be tested for sugar content at the first racking. A new wine usually does not taste good and the taste test may be fallible at the time of the first racking. If a wine has not fermented to completion at the first racking it is usually necessary to reinoculate with a new yeast culture.

While some people prefer sweet wines, and the taste test should dictate what a wine drinker drinks, it should be remembered that high-sugar, low-alcohol wines may start to ferment again in the bottle. If this occurs in ordinary wine bottles, the bottles may explode. A sugar analysis warns the wine maker of any such danger that exists.

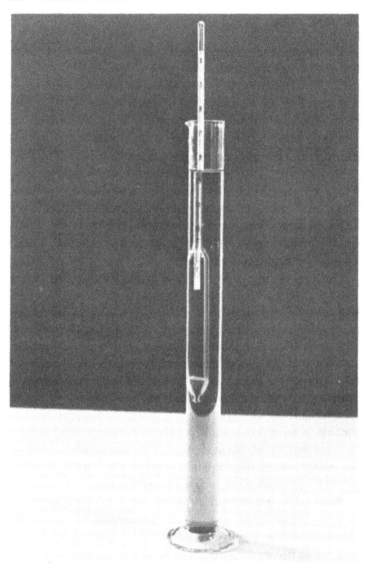

21. A hydrometer floats in a cylinder of fresh must. Hydrometers are used both to determine the sugar content of a must and the alcoholic content of a mead.

Hydrometers

A hydrometer is an instrument based on the fact that an object will sink in a liquid to the point that its weight is displaced. Alcohol is less dense than water, and as the alcoholic content is increased the hydrometer sinks deeper into the liquid. Sugars and other solids add to the density and as they increase the hydrometer rises.

It is simple enough to make an accurate measurement of the components of a liquid that consists of alcohol and water only, or of sugar and water only. However, when other materials are present they confuse the readings, and the hydrometer becomes less useful. One cannot measure the alcoholic content of a wine or mead without clearing away extraneous materials through distillation. However, a hydrometer is reasonably accurate for measuring the quantity of sugar in the diluted honey before fermenting the mead.

Alcohol

Making an analysis for the amount of alcohol in a wine (or any other alcoholic beverage) is easy enough once one has the equipment and a little background information. The amount of alcohol in a solution may be determined with a device called a hydrometer. In principle, this is the same gadget used to determine the freezing point of water or of the solution in a car radiator. The problem is that the hydrometer is also affected by the amount of sugar and other materials in solution in the wine. Even though one determines the alcoholic content of a wine correctly, it is not probable that the same reading by a hydrometer in a second wine will have an equal value. This is true because the quantity of the other materials in solution varies from wine to wine.

Therefore, to determine the amount of alcohol in a wine one must get the alcohol out of the wine and into a water solution. This is done by distillation. The distilled product may be placed in a glass cylinder and the hydrometer introduced. The hydrometer must not rest on the bottom of the cylinder, and there must be solution all around the hydrometer so it floats freely. Most hydrometers are sold with the proper size cylinder for making the final reading. Most alcohol hydrometers and cylinders for wine are made to determine the alcohol in one hundred cubic centimeters (100 c.c. or 100 ml.) of distilled materials, and are calibrated to read accurately at a specific temperature. For the purposes of the home wine maker, a slight temperature variation is of little consequence, but one should be aware that this is a fact.

The first step in determining an alcoholic concentration is to measure accurately 100 c.c. of the wine to be tested. This may be done with a graduated cylinder but it is more accurately done with a volumetric flask. A volumetric flask has a large base or bulb with a long narrow neck with only one calibration on about the middle of the neck.

The measured 100 c.c. of wine are added to a distillation flask. More water is added, usually 50 to 100 c.c., but the quantity of this water is not important. In making the analysis, one wants to distill 100 or almost 100 c.c. of material. Without adding water before the distillation, the residue of the wine would stick to the inside of the distillation flask. Since the alcohol distills rapidly, more so than water, it is assumed that all the alcohol one can obtain from a distillation is evaporated by the time 100 c.c., or almost that volume, is distilled from the distillation flask.

A condenser is also required for a distillation. Condensers are simple to run and observe. A condenser is a glass coil encased in a larger cylinder through which one may pass cool, running water. The wine is heated in the distilling flask, causing evaporated materal to rise and pass into the coil, where the volatile alcohol and water are cooled and condensed. One may see where the colorless liquid (alcohol and water) is condensing in the glass coil. It is usually advisable to regulate the heat to control the condensation. The volatile liquid should be forced to condense in about the middle of the coil.

The condensate is collected in the 100 c.c. volumetric flask. Usually only 98 or 99 c.c. are collected in the flask, since the last few drops may flow so fast as to overfill it, and if one is forced to throw away some of the distilled liquid, one will also be throwing away alcohol. It is better to underdistill and to fill the flask with water. By the time one has distilled 98 or 99 c.c. of material it is logical to assume that all the alcohol has been evaporated, and adding water has no adverse effect.

The equipment needed, then, for an alcohol analysis is as follows: a hotplate or heat source with a variable control; a hydrometer and cylinder of 100 c.c. capacity; a volumetric flask to measure 100 c.c. or whatever volume is required for the hydrometer; a distillation flask of 300 to 500 c.c. capacity, the larger volume being best; a condenser, tubing, and corks for the connection between the distillation flask and the condenser; and rubber tubing to pass a slow flow of water through the condenser. The temperature of the condenser may be checked by holding one's hand on it, or, better, by observing the material condensing within the glass coil.

An alcoholic analysis usually requires 15 to 20 minutes to make.[1] The equipment will cost $15 to $30, but is usually a satisfying investment.

---

[1] Measuring alcohol by weight and volume: The facts suggest that methods of measuring alcohol were designed to confuse the public. While this may not be precisely true, it is certainly a fact that there are several methods of measuring the alcoholic content of a beverage. These include proof, alcohol by volume, and alcohol by weight. The first fact to understand is that equal volumes of water and alcohol do not weigh the same; alcohol weighs less than an equal volume of water.

Proof is twice alcohol, but alcohol by volume, not weight. Thus, a proof of 80 means that the alcoholic content of a beverage is 40 per cent, but 40 per cent by volume. If the same beverage was measured in terms of its alcoholic content by weight, there would be only about 33 per cent alcohol present.

At the level of beer, where the term proof is not used, it is said that a beer might contain five per cent alcohol by volume. If beer makers were to express the alcoholic content of their product by weight, they would be forced to say only four per cent alcohol was present. Since everyone wants more for his money, the designation of the alcohol content of a beverage by its higher figure, proof for whiskey, gin, and fortified wines, and percentage by volume for wines and beers, is preferred. The buyer is forced to understand the system!

Total solids in a must

Fruit juice contains sugar and two to three per cent of other materials in solution. It is important to know how much sugar is present in the must. If too little sugar is present the wine will be low in alcohol and will not keep well.

Total solids are measured by a hydrometer. A home wine maker should purchase one that reads from about 12 to 25 per cent balling (= brix). The reading on the stem of the hydro-meter will, in effect, be equivalent to the per cent of sugar in the wine. It is probably advisable to buy one's hydrometer for measuring sugar from a wine supply shop, to make certain it was not calibrated for other purposes. Directions accompany-ing the instrument should indicate any corrections necessary for various musts and temperatures. Hydrometers are calibrated for specific temperatures and correction factors must be applied in some instances. The directions should also indicate how to read the instrument when it is in the liquid. Since any liquid has a tendency to "climb" anything put into it, a meniscus (a concave or convex section) is formed around the stem of the hydrometer. One reads the value on the stem of the hydrometer at the bottom of the meniscus, not at the top.

The ideal balling reading on a hydrometer for wine is 22 to 24 per cent. Wines with a balling reading above about 28 per cent do not ferment well. Yeasts in the genus *Saccharomyces* are not acclimated to higher sugar concentrations.

Hydrometers are delicate instruments that break easily and may give a false reading if they are dirty. They should be washed clean after each use and dried with a clean cloth. It is advisable to have a special box or drawer in which they may be kept.

Measuring pH

Under laboratory conditions, the pH of a wine is measured accurately with a pH meter. Such instruments cost several hundred dollars and require constant attention to remain in good condition. Fortunately, one may also measure the pH of a liquid with a special paper, usually sold in tape form, that shows the correct pH colorometrically. The accuracy is within reason, usually 0.2 to 0.4 of a pH unit. Since a pH between 3 and 4 is suitable for a fermentation, this is sufficiently accurate. To measure the pH, a piece of the sensitive paper is dipped into the liquid and compared immediately with the color guide provided with the pH paper.

Since measuring the pH of a juice or wine is not too common, not all of the shops that cater to home wine makers stock pH paper. However, such papers are available from chemical supply houses, or a local druggist should be able to obtain them without difficulty. The pH papers are available to measure a wide range of sensitivity, but the home wine maker should choose one that is sensitive in the pH range of 3 to 5.

Total and volatile acidity

In making wine there is concern over total acid and volatile acid. These are two distinct considerations. As indicated elsewhere, acid in wine is necessary for the development of the proper flavor. Measuring total acid is a relatively simple matter. One adds base to an acid solution that contains a dye showing a color at the proper pH. The volatile acid content of a wine is included in the overall total acid value. Most wines should have total acid values in the vicinity of 0.5 to 0.7 per cent; musts will have slightly higher values since some acid is lost during the fermentation.

Volatile acid is another matter. A small value for volatile acid is expected in a wine. A high volatile acid value indicates spoilage, usually because of *Acetobacter* and the production of acetic acid. Federal regulations state a white wine should contain not more than 0.12 per cent volatile acid, and red wines should not have more than 0.14 per cent. The better wines will

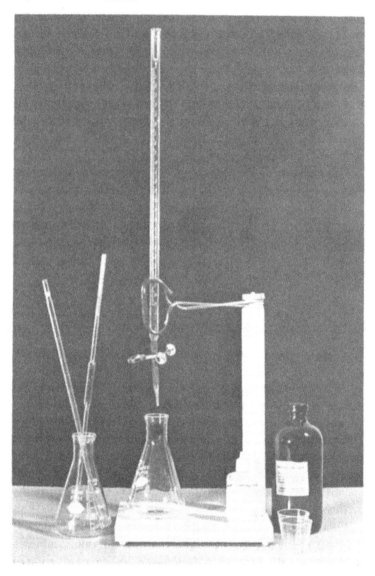

22. *The equipment needed for titration is shown. A home laboratory serves as a guide to the making of better mead. Photo by E. S. Phillips.*

have a volatile acid content equal to about half of these values. Volatile acid may be measured in the home laboratory. The equipment required to do so is a little more elaborate than that used for total acidity, but the techniques are not impossible. Like so many processes, the whole thing is very simple once one has all the background information and has run through the process a few times.

The procedure for measuring total acidity is the same for a must or a wine. Directions usually accompany the kits sold in home wine shops for measuring total acidity. The procedure is as follows: Usually ten milliliters (equals c.c. or cubic centimeters) of wine are measured into a beaker, preferably with a volumetric pipette so that the measurement is accurate. A buret, a long tube with a glass petcock, is used to drop a base, NaOH (sodium hydroxide), into the wine. Phenolphthalein, a dye that turns pink at pH 7, is added before the titration; only a few drops of phenolphthalein are necessary and one needs to see only a lasting light pink color to end the so-called titration. The amount of base required to reach pH 7 indicates the total acid present. This value may be obtained from the tables that accompany the kits sold for this purpose.

Measuring volatile acid requires a special distillation apparatus, including a 1,000-milliliter flask and a Liebig condenser. The condensate is titrated as above with phenolphthalein as the color indicator. Since volatile acid is principally acetic acid, and sometimes to a lesser extent butyric acid, both of which have distinctive odors, the first of vinegar and the second of rancid butter, most home wine makers generally depend upon their noses to tell them whether the wine is good or not. Measurements are precise; the nose is not. However, with experience one can develop a good nose for good wines. Volatile acid is obviously undesirable. The proper attention to sanitation and the use of sulfur dioxide gives the protection most home wine makers need to prevent high volatile acid values. Total acid, similarly, is a matter of taste; this too can be reasonably judged by the trained palate.

23. Judging mead at an Eastern Apicultural Honey Show. Here the judge examines for clarity. Photo by A. Delicata. 24. The judge smells a cork, which can tell him much about the quality of the mead. Photo by A. Delicata.

Judging mead

Mead was rare in honey shows ten years ago. Today, as county fairs become more popular and interest in beekeeping increases, there are classes for mead in many shows. Often there will be exhibits in at least five categories: dry and sweet mead, dry and sweet fruit mead, and sparkling mead. Many different fruits are being used in making meads, making it impossible to have a class for each combination; this often makes judging difficult.

It is regrettable that more people do not submit their mead in competition. I think it is important, however, to enter only shows that require the judge to use a score card. This forces the judge to assign points in various categories so the exhibitor can understand the grading and learn from the process. Most judges will also make useful comments if a card is available to them. The card used by the Eastern Apicultural Society is shown in figure 25. Using a scorecard at home helps the mead maker to

25. One type of judge's score card. One should not enter a contest where the judge does not assign points to various categories so that the contestants may profit from the experience.

EASTERN APICULTURAL SOCIETY		JUDGE'S SCORE CARD	
MEAD		Class _____	Entry No. _____

Points	Scoring	Item	Judge's remarks
5		Color	
10		Clarity	
25		Bouquet	
60		Flavor, balance and quality	
100		Award:	

taste his mead systematically and to think more carefully about where improvements might be made.

It is understood that no two people would agree precisely on the points to be considered. Listed below are considerations most often mentioned by judges.

Appearance, Clarity, Color, and Sweetness

The values assigned for these four characteristics will vary, depending on such factors as the age and type of mead. However, it is generally agreed that a bright mead has a greater eye appeal than a dull mead. A cloudy mead may have good flavor, but one's expectations are more likely to be fulfilled if the eyes, as well as the taste buds, are stimulated.

Wine and mead connoisseurs usually do not favor sweet meads. It is true that sugar has been used throughout history to cover for mead makers' mistakes, and this, in itself, may guide experienced people away from sweet meads. It is also correct that many subtle qualities of a beverage are apparent only if there is little sugar. Unfortunately, many people with whom I've talked automatically think, just because it is based on honey, mead should be sweet; this is certainly not the case.

Bouquet, Odor, and Aroma

One of the more important characteristics of a wine or mead is a pleasant bouquet. It is difficult, if not impossible, to describe a preferred bouquet, though experienced mead makers are aware that the bouquet of mead differs distinctly from that of grape wines. Odor and aroma are words often used interchangeably with bouquet and it is not totally inappropriate to do so.

One should become familiar with the vinegary smell associated with an acetic acid fermentation. Bad odors can also result from the use of moldy barrels. Meads made from burned honeys, especially those melted in the presence of wax, are easy to detect. Yeastiness is easily detected and is evident in meads that are consumed when too young. Bottles with poor closures may reveal themselves through a bland bouquet or, occasionally, a total lack of bouquet.

Flavor, Balance, and Quality

In discussing flavor we are concerned not only with one's immediate impression, but also the aftertaste. The two are different. Since most meads are consumed with a meal, it is important that the flavor be such that it compliments food. Bitterness, astringency, tartness, and similarly offensive tastes are to be avoided. Aging does much to eliminate these undesirable characteristics through the very slow-paced chemical process.

In the final analysis, a fine mead is one that one enjoys consuming and that causes guests to make kind remarks. It is not difficult to make good mead today. The biology and chemistry of the process have been studied at length: We know how to avoid contamination with undesirable microbes; good yeasts are readily available. Perhaps the most difficult element is time, for which there is no substitute. All too often one has too little of the best mead and too much of the inferior; care in making the mead will eliminate many of the poorer products.

Index

acetic acid, 121, 125
Acetobacter, 108-109, 119
Adam, Brother, 60-61
aging, 75-77
alcohol analysis, 115-117
aluminum, 110
American Wine Society, 10
ammonium phosphate, 58
ammonium sulphate, 62
antifoam, 54-56, 59
apple juice, 64
ash, 30
Asiatic ginger, 63

barrels, 37-40
Beck, B.F., 22
beer, 56
best yeast for mead, 45
Bevan, E., 21
biotin, 62
boiling the honey-water, 20, 59, 65-67, 111
bottles, 80-91
bottling, 80
Bower, L., 10
Brand melter, 32
brood in mead making, 31

calcium pantothenate, 62
camomile, 63
cappings honey, 32
capsules, 92
carbon dioxide, 13-14, 94
carboys, 37-40
cardomon seed, 63
casein, 78-79
cellar temperature, 42-43
champagne, 15, 69, 75, 80, 94-96
charcoal, 104-105
Child, F. J., 16
chilling, 77, 111
cider, 64
cinnamon, 61,63
citric acid, 58, 62
clorox, 35-36
closures, 80
cloudiness, 77
cloves, 18-19, 20, 61, 63
Comer, P., 37-38, 90
copper, 110
corks, 9, 80, 85-91, 104, 108

corkscrews, 91
cream of tartar, 58
crown caps, 9, 83-85, 100, 102
Cruess, W.V., 58
crystallized honey, 28, 30
cyser, 22

Delicata, A., 122
Digbie, K., 18
diseases, 107
disgorging sparkling mead, 101-105
disorders, 107
Drambouie, 24
dried yeast cultures, 50-51
drinking sparkling meads, 105-106

East African beer, 31-32
Eastern Apicultural Society, 123
ecology of yeast cell growth, 47
egg albumin, 78-79
extrafloral nectaries, 26

fennel-root, 20
fermentation values, 40-42
fermenting, 68-70
Filippelo, F., 58
filtering, 77
filtration of honey, 31
Finger Lakes Honey Producers
    Cooperative, 16
fining, 77
foils, 92
French, B., 10
fructose, 27
fruit meads, 64

Gayre, G.R., 21-22
gelatin, 78-79
gin, 15
ginger, 18-19
glucose, 27
glucose-fructose ratio, 28
glucose oxidase, 27-28
glycerin, 88
grape juice, 21, 48
growth factors in honey, 30

headspace, 56, 82-83
herbs, 62-63
hippocras, 23
home analysis, 112
honey, 27-28, 30-31, 33

hops, 19, 21, 65
hydromel, 20, 23
hydrometers, 114-116, 118
hyssop, 63

inositol, 62
invertase, 27
Irish Mist, 24
iron, 67, 110
isinglass, 78-79

Johnston, J.W., Jr., 63
judging mead, 112, 123-125
jugs, 37-40

keeping quality of honey, 33
Krupnik, 24

labels, 92-93
lemon mint, 63

Macdonell, A., 18
magnesium chloride, 62
Marsh, G.L., 58
meads that will not clear, 77-79
melomel, 23
metallic cloudiness, 110
metallic contamination, 67
metheglin, 22, 62-63
Morse, G.D., 9
Morse-Steinkraus Patent, 61
mousy, 110

names for mead, 22-23
nectar, 26
Norsemen, 17
nutmeg, 63
nutrients, 13

oak, 39, 60, 86
osmophilic yeasts, 51-52

parsley-root, 20
Pasteur, 12, 96, 110
pasteurization, 77
peptone, 62
Pfund grader, 32
pH, 13, 28, 47-48, 50, 64, 118-119
phenolphthalein, 121
Phillips, E.S., 10, 55-56, 72, 99, 120
plastic, 39
pollen, 26, 30-31
potassium metabisulfite, 53-54
potassium phosphate, 62
primary fermentation, 69-70
proof, 15, 117
protein precipitate, 110-111
pymeat, 22

pyridoxine, 62

racking, 68, 71-74
recipes, 18-20
residual sugar, 113
retsina, 14
Robin Hood, 16-17
Rohn, O., 9
ropiness in mead, 109
rose hips, 63
rosemary, 19, 63

Saccharomyces cerviseae, 46
sack mead, 22
sack metheglin, 22
sanitation, 20, 35-37
screw caps, 83
secondary fermentation, 70
sodium bisulfite, 53-54
sodium hydrogen sulphate, 62
sparkling mead, 70, 94-106
spiced meads, 12
spices, 18-20, 62-63
Steinkraus, K.H., 9, 10, 61, 92
stuck meads, 74-75
sucrose, 27
sulfiting, 53-54
sulfur, 36-37, 53-54
sulfur candles, 36-37
sulfur dioxide, 36, 40, 42, 54, 59, 60, 71, 81, 83-85, 88
sulfur dioxide tablets, 36
sweet basil, 63
sweet woodruff, 63
sweetening sparkling mead, 101-105

tannin, 78-79, 111
tartaric acid, 58
temperature control, 34, 42-43
thiamine, 62
thyme, 63
tin, 110
total acid, 119-121

urea, 58
urine-sugar analysis sets, 113

vinegar, 57, 108-109
volatile acidity, 119-121

washing soda, 36
whiskey, 15

yeast, 60
yeast cells, 46-47
yeast starters, 48

zinc, 67

Printed in the USA
CPSIA information can be obtained
at www.ICGtesting.com
CBHW051151151023
1350CB00002B/6